THE WESTERN FILMS OF
JOHN FORD

THE WESTERN FILMS OF

JOHN FORD

by J. A. Place

THE CITADEL PRESS   Secaucus, N.J.

Dedicated to Nick

First edition
Copyright © 1974 by J. A. Place
All rights reserved
Published by Citadel Press
A division of Lyle Staart, Inc.
120 Enterprise Ave., Secaucus, N. J. 07094
In Canada: George J. McLeod Limited
73 Bathurst St., Toronto, Ont.
Manufactured in the United States of America

Designed by A. Christopher Simon
Library of Congress catalog card number: 74-80827
ISBN 0-8065-0445-5

ACKNOWLEDGMENTS

Stills: Eddie Brandt, British Film Institute, Collectors' Book Store, Mark Haggard, Robert Herrup, Larry Edmunds Bookshop, Blake Lucas, Alain Silver.

I am indebted to Mark Haggard, David Chierichetti, and David Bradley for their assistance on this project. To Jim Kitses, who nurtured my interest in Westerns in general and Ford in particular, I am grateful specifically for the ideas that form the basis of the chapter on *Drums Along the Mohawk*. I thank the UCLA Film Archive for arranging a screening of *My Darling Clementine*. For encouragement throughout the project I thank all of the above and Heidi Fletcher, Sylvia Harvey, and Eugene Archer. Above all, I thank L. S. Peterson, who compiled the credits and who read and made editorial suggestions on the manuscript in all stages of its development.

CONTENTS

THE WESTERN FILMS OF
JOHN FORD

1
Introduction

John Ford directing, 1959.

Stagecoach, 1939.

The greatest value of art lies in its ability to express feelings, its capacity to move one's emotions. Whether it is expressed through a Bach chorale, a Leonardo painting, a Michelangelo statue, a Donne poem, or a Shakespeare drama, a work's only claim to being an artistic masterpiece lies in its power to elicit emotional responses from people of every generation since it was created.

The popular arts of our age are music and film, and both in their finest forms appeal to emotions. The impoverishment of painting, sculpture, theater, and literature as art forms in the twentieth century has been brought about by the abstraction of emotion into intellectual and scientific expression. Thus, in the current vogue of regarding cinema as art, the conspicuously "intellectual" films are often those which are most honored, since they are most like other "respectable" art forms today.

Even within this framework, the films of John Ford are among the most highly regarded American films; yet meaningful criticism has yet to be written on his work. With few exceptions, articles and books about his career are anecdotal, descriptive, or venerative without being critical, insightful, or illuminating. Perhaps this is because John Ford's films move people emotionally more than challenge them intellectually, and it is difficult to write coldly and analytically about the profound experiencing of these films. This experience cannot be communicated through the written word, regardless of its evocative power; the films must be seen. The purpose of this work is to examine the emotions Ford creates in his Westerns.

John Ford worked in the motion-picture industry almost from its very beginnings. Although his films cover a number of varied subjects—Westerns, historical dramas, comedies, romances, detective films, political pictures—they represent a unified body of work of an acutely sensitive artistic consciousness. There is a world view in his work that deepens and develops throughout his career, that reflects and

John Ford, 1937.

John Ford, 1970.

4

filters through his artistic vision the mythology of modern America.

The point should be made here that movies are a collaborative medium. It is impossible to consider one man the absolute creator of a film, be he John Ford or Ingmar Bergman. Innumerable hands touch and affect the finished product, and no matter how much a director is in control, he does not make every decision on every aspect of the work as would a painter, writer, or composer. This may seem to indicate that one cannot accurately discuss "the films of John Ford," but quite the reverse is true. When, in chaotic circumstances such as the making of a movie, one man's vision emerges to such an extent that the films in which he has been involved bear his artistic imprint, one must assume that they are his films. While it is useless to argue minor points and touches, such as a line of dialogue or a camera angle, the only conditions under which film criticism can be an evaluation of art, and not of craft or sociology, are those which assume one artistic consciousness behind the work.

There is an intentionality behind a work of art. In the case of Ford's films, if it is not totally accurate to call that intentionality "John Ford," it is at least convenient. No one familiar with the body of his work could deny that Ford's personal vision makes up the bulk of the intentionality of his movies, so that for our purposes, that intentionality will be referred to as John Ford.

There are many ways to approach that body of work which is John Ford's Westerns. Although the great power of his films comes from his personal vision, it is significant that they are rooted in American history and set in the genre of the Western.

The West in American thought, politics, and art is a profound and often ambiguous force. For a detailed analysis of its effect, see Henry Nash Smith's excellent *Virgin Land: The American West As Symbol and Myth.* For our purposes, suffice it to say that the concept of the West embodies conflicting ideals. On the one hand it represents essentially antisocial, individual, and solitary values through which a man can escape the implicitly corrupting influence of society. On the other, the West represents a pure, natural, fertile wilderness in which the society of man can build a new community based on the cleansing, healing effects of nature. These conflicting ideals are present in growing tension through John Ford's entire body of films, both Westerns and non-Westerns.

Philosophical views of American history are the intellectual background for the Western genre and its special significance for Americans, but more important to understanding the emotional impact of Westerns is the element of myth they contain. Myths are universal patterns of human experience. In his Westerns, John Ford re-creates those myths which are most meaningful to him and uses ritual (much as religion uses it) to restate the personal and cultural values contained within the myths.

Rituals are formal, sometimes stylized re-enactments of very basic patterns for dealing with fearful or awesome human experience. In his films, Ford establishes personal patterns of these experiences—dances, weddings, births, funerals, honor, and above all, sacrifice. We respond to these rituals with emotion, and from the emotional experiences we take gratification. Even when story lines are cliché and predictable, the working out of insoluble tensions and frustrations through fantasy helps to relieve similar tensions in our own lives.

Thus, a work of art functions for a society as a dream functions for an individual—it expresses through shared patterns of myth and ritual the irreconcilable needs and desires that the society must repress, thereby relieving some of the tension such repression causes. Recurring myths are the expression of man's collective unconscious, and their constant expression and reinterpretation is the art of the society.

The Western, then, is defined by its relation to myth through its use of ritual and dream, its culturally shared background of the American dream and by its forms and conventions. It repeats and reaffirms cultural and universal experience. On the artistic level, however, the dream is subject to reinterpretation and change, even to fundamental questioning of the dream while still affirming the cultural values inherent in it.

Tension and ambiguity, most cogently expressed in Ford's richest films, provide the energy and conflict from which arises the great emotional involvement of these movies. The most basic tension is between the individual and the community, which is perhaps the basic dichotomy expressed in art of all forms. In Ford's films characters often feel a great need to serve the community, to become one with it, yet to hold their individuality somewhat apart from it. This is perhaps why the themes of both American politics and the settling of the American West are so conducive to expressing this theme. In both, the *individual* actions of men integrate them into the structure of a better society while the very individuality of those actions sets them apart.

This is the fundamental dichotomy of American populism (as expressed by Thoreau and Walt Whitman)—building a perfect society of man through the individual efforts of individual men, whose explicit value will be rendered meaningless by the creation of that society. What Ford arrived at in his later films was that the implicit value of the individual was greater than any that could be achieved through the creation of the pure society. The individual of *Drums Along the Mohawk* could put on and take off his uniform—the transformation from individual to part

Rio Grande, 1950.

Changing interpretation of the Wyatt Earp myth: *My Darling Clementine,* 1946, and *Cheyenne Autumn,* 1964.

of a functioning unit was not significant. This is less and less the case in the military pictures, in which the need to bend one's individual will to the military necessity becomes harder and harder to bear and finally, with *The Horse Soldiers* and then *Two Rode Together,* becomes of less value than individual priorities.

Ford used both the military and the domestic unit as metaphors for the community. Thus, *How Green Was My Valley,* set in Wales, is concerned more with a community and a family disintegrating than with any national themes, and is emotionally closer to *Cheyenne Autumn* than to *The Quiet Man. Fort Apache* achieves much of its meaning and emotion

The solitary individual: *She Wore a Yellow Ribbon.*

6

through the almost perfect integration of the elements of family and military in the O'Rourke family. And *Cheyenne Autumn* derives its spare emotional value from a total application of the concept of community as extended family.

Sacrifice is a very strong and increasingly ambiguous concept in Ford's Westerns. In many of the early films, people must die for anything of value to be achieved. People die so that others may live, so that the building of the society can continue. When the general dies just as Martin "comes to life" in *Drums Along the Mohawk,* the connection is made quite clear, and although there is no question about the greater good of the sacrifice, Ford makes the loss

The young farming family: *Drums Along the Mohawk,* 1939.

The extended military family: *Fort Apache,* 1948.

The shell of the military family: *The Horse Soldiers,* 1959.

deeply felt and it militates against the joy of renewed life in Lana and Martin.

In *Fort Apache,* the sacrifice of Colonel Thursday is seen with nostalgia, reverence, and a strong sense that his sacrifice is right, for the greater good of the cavalry unit. The value of his sacrifice is made explicit in the epilogue sequence, in which the spirit of the cavalry marches on outside the window as Colonel York watches, holding within himself the secret of Colonel Thursday.

In *My Darling Clementine* and *The Searchers* the idea of civilians sacrificing to build a better society is most evident, expressed verbally in *The Searchers* in the "Texican" speech when Mrs. Jorgensen says "if [this country] needs our bones in the ground before it is a better place ..." and the connection between ritual sacrifice and achieving a greater good is unquestionable.

In all Ford's films, however, there is nostalgia both for whatever must be sacrificed and for an individual who does not give up his individuality, his isolation from the group. Indeed, his separate and observing quality interprets the value of the society. In the early films, the tension of the individual and his relation to the whole can be left unresolved, because Ford has not yet seen the dichotomy as irreconcilable. Even in *Three Bad Men,* perhaps Ford's earliest dark film, in which three good "bad" men give up their lives for the family unit of a young farming couple and are then remembered in the couple's son, the tension is not acute.

But it is evident even in these early films that Ford's real commitment is to the individual, to the character outside the society for which he is working. When his sacrifice is required for the continuation of

Sacrifice: the death of the general in *Drums Along the Mohawk.*

The ritual of death: the burial of the Southern general in *She Wore a Yellow Ribbon.*

that society, as in *The Searchers* and *The Man Who Shot Liberty Valance,* the tension becomes unbearable and Ford creates his most existential films. In both these Westerns (as in many Ford non-Westerns of this period, most notably *Seven Women*), the individual who embodies the values that create the better society must be destroyed or banished in order for that society to grow. The tensions of that destruction become existential because although Ford by this time no longer believes in the transcendent value of the society, he does adhere to acting out the ritual of affirmation for the society.

All Ford's Westerns, as early as *Straight Shooting* and as late as *Cheyenne Autumn,* are a ritual affirma-tion of the society they represent and grow from. The maturation process is one of disillusionment with the society while retaining the rituals as existential values within themselves.

The individual, then, is at the heart of Ford's view of the world. In his early films a man's society could justify his existence, but by his late films nothing remains but the ritual of action and sacrifice to give meaning to the life of the alienated individual. *Cheyenne Autumn* is Ford's blackest film because the sacrifice is made, but the community and the individual are combined into one entity and there is nothing left for the ritual to affirm.

Ford on the set of *How The West Was Won,* 1962, for which he directed the Civil War sequence.

2
THE SILENT WESTERNS:

STRAIGHT SHOOTING (1917)

CREDITS

Production company, Universal-Butterfly. *Director,* Jack Ford. *Script,* George Hively. *Director of photography,* George Scott. *Released August 27, 1917. Length,* five reels. *Working titles,* THE CATTLE WAR; JOAN OF THE CATTLE COUNTRY. *Rereleased in two-reel version,* STRAIGHT SHOOTING, *January 1925. Distributor,* Universal.

CAST

Harry Carey *(Cheyenne Harry),* Molly Malone *(Joan Sims),* Duke Lee *("Thunder" Flint),* Vester Pegg *("Placer" Fremont),* Hoot Gibson *(Danny Morgan),* George Berrell *(Sweetwater Sims),* Ted Brooks *(Ted Sims),* Milt Brown *(Black-Eyed Pete).*

SYNOPSIS:

Harry is an outlaw hired by ranchers to murder farmers. However, when he sees the Sims family grieving over the body of Ted Sims, killed by Placer Fremont, with whom Harry got drunk the day before, he changes sides. After killing Fremont in a street showdown, he gets Black-Eyed Pete and his boys, an outlaw gang Harry used to ride with, to come to the farmers' aid. The farmers win the battle, and Harry stays, presumably to marry Joan Sims.

THE IRON HORSE (1924)

CREDITS

Production company, Fox ("A John Ford Production"). *Director,* John Ford. *Script,* Charles Kenyon. *Story,* Charles Kenyon, John Russell. *Directors of photography,* George Schneiderman, Burnett Guffey. *Titles,* Charles Darnton. *Music score,* Erno Rapee. *Released (with tinted sequences) August 28, 1924. Length,* 11,335 feet. *Running time,* approximately 165 minutes. *Distributor,* Fox.

Straight Shooting, The Iron Horse, Three Bad Men

CAST

George O'Brien (*Davy Brandon*), Madge Bellamy (*Miriam Marsh*), Judge Charles Edward Bull (*Abraham Lincoln*), Will Walling (*Thomas Marsh*), Fred Kohler (*Bauman*), Cyril Chadwick (*Peter Jesson*), Gladys Hulette (*Ruby*), James Marcus (*Judge Haller*), Francis Powers (*Sergeant Slattery*), J. Farrell McDonald (*Corporal Casey*), James Welch (*Private Schultz*), Colin Chase (*Tony*), Jack O'Brien (*Dinny*), Walter Rogers (*General Dodge*), George Wagner (*Colonel "Buffalo Bill" Cody*), John Padjan (*Wild Bill Hickok*), Charles O'Malley (*Major North*), Charles Newton (*Collis Huntington*), Delbert Mann (*Charles Crocker*), Chief Big Tree (*Cheyenne Chief*), Chief White Spear (*Sioux Chief*), Edward Piel (*old Chinese man*), James Gordon (*Dave Brandon, Sr.*), Winston Miller (*Davy, age ten*), Peggy Cartwright (*Miriam, age eight*), Thomas C. Durant (*Jack Ganzhorn*), Stanhope Wheatcroft (*John Hay*), Frances Teague (*Polka Dot*), Dan Borzage, Clark Gable, *Jupiter*, of the old Central Pacific and *119*, of the old Union Pacific. Also, "A Regiment of United States troops and cavalry; 3,000 Railway Workmen; 1,000 Chinese laborers; 800 Pawnee, Sioux, and Cheyenne Indians; 2,800 horses; 1,300 buffalo; 10,000 Texas steers."

SYNOPSIS:

In the middle of the nineteenth century, the transcontinental railroad is a dream in the mind of David Brandon, endorsed by Abraham Lincoln. Brandon and his son Davy set out to find the railroad passage, and Davy witnesses Brandon's murder by Indians led by a man with three fingers at the site of a spectacular pass.

A decade later, Davy is a Pony Express rider. He escapes from Indians by leaping on a train moving on the first part of the transcontinental railroad being built by Thomas Marsh, the father of Davy's childhood sweetheart, Miriam. He and Miriam are reunited, but she is engaged to Peter Jesson, an Eastern surveyor working for her father to find a pass for the railroad. Davy tries to show him the pass he and his father found so long ago, but Jesson is really working for Bauman, the owner of a large ranch, who stands to profit if the railroad goes through his land instead of through the pass. Jesson tries unsuccessfully to kill Davy, who returns to learn that Bauman is the three-fingered "Indian" who killed his father. Davy exposes Bauman and goes to work on the other end of the railroad. When the east and west lines meet, Davy and Miriam are finally joined again.

THREE BAD MEN (1926)

CREDITS

Production company, Fox. *Director*, John Ford. *Script*, John Stone; based on Herman Whittaker's novel OVER THE BORDER. *Director of photography*, George Schneiderman. *Locations filmed at Jackson Hole, Wyoming, and in the Mojave Desert. Released (with tinted sequences) October 17, 1926. Length*, 8,000 feet. *Running time*, approximately 92 minutes. *Distributor*, Fox.

CAST

George O'Brien (*Dan O'Malley*), Olive Borden (*Lee Carlton*), J. Farrell McDonald (*Mike Costigan*), Tom Santschi (*Bull Stanley*), Frank Campeau (*Spade Allen*), Lou Tellegen (*Sheriff Layne Hunter*), George Harris (*Joe Minsk*), Jay Hunt (*old prospector*), Priscilla Bonner (*Millie Stanley*), Otis Harlan (*Zack Leslie*), Walter Perry (*Pat Monahan*), Grace Gordon (*Millie's friend*), Alec B. Francis (*the Reverend Calvin Benson*), George Irving (*General Neville*), Phyllis Haver (*Prairie Beauty*).

SYNOPSIS:

In the 1870s, immigrants and pioneers travel west in search of gold and Indian lands to be given away in the land rush of 1876. A Kentucky colonel and his daughter Lee head for the Dakotas with their thoroughbreds. They meet Dan O'Malley, a young Irishman, who flirts with Lee and helps them fix a wagon wheel. After Dan goes his way, three bad men try to steal the horses, but the sheriff of "Custer," Layne Hunter, sends men who beat them to it and kill Colonel Carlton. The three bad men ride up preparing to kill those remaining, but when Bull sees Lee, they pretend to have saved her from Hunter's men and hire on (without pay) as her men.

Bull's sister Millie has gone off with Hunter on the promise of marriage, but Layne refuses to marry her and even "gives" her to another man. She sees her brother, who is searching for her, but in her shame will not let him find her. During this time, Bull decides Lee should have a husband, and he finds Dan, who also hires on with Lee. Finally Bull leads a revolt against Hunter, whose men burn down the church full of women and children. Bull, Dan, and the townspeople rescue them, but Millie is shot and dies in Bull's arms.

During the gold rush, Layne's men wait across the line and follow Lee and her men, because Dan has a gold map given to him by an old prospector Layne's men killed. One by one the three bad men die to ward off Hunter's men, with Bull finally killing Layne and dying himself. Years later, Dan and Lee, with a baby named for the three, are seen still protected by their friends.

Johm Ford came to Hollywood in 1914, fresh out of high school, to work in the motion-picture industry. He began as a laborer, an assistant prop man, and worked his way into writing and directing shorts, none of which has survived. In 1917 he directed his first feature, *Straight Shooting*. He continued to make silent films until 1929, when he made his first feature-length talkie, *The Black Watch*. During those twelve years, Ford directed about sixty silent films, more than two-thirds of them Westerns. Only three of the silent Westerns exist today—*Straight Shooting, The Iron Horse*, and *Three Bad Men*. *The Iron Horse* is considered a classic of the silent film and was Ford's first real success, but both *Straight Shooting* and *Three Bad Men* more directly anticipate his later masterpieces.

John Ford and photographer
George Schneiderman on *The
Iron Horse*, 1924.

Scenes from an unindentified Ford directed silent with
Harry Carey.

Spade Allen (Frank Campeau), Bull Stanley (Tom Santschi), Mike Costigan (J. Farrell McDonald), and Dan O'Malley (George O'Brien) in *Three Bad Men,* 1926.

Harry Carey as Cheyenne Harry in *Straight Shooting,* 1917.

The first shot of Cheyenne Harry: the man and the wanted poster.

While both *The Iron Horse* and *Three Bad Men* are "epic" films of the settling of the American West, *Straight Shooting* is a simple movie about ranchers, farmers, and an outlaw who sides with the farmers in a range war. What is most interesting about *Straight Shooting,* in terms of Ford's later Westerns, is that many elements appear in this first little feature in essentially final, well-developed form—elements that will remain important visual motifs and themes of later, more sophisticated works. Most striking of these is his use of landscape. Throughout his career Ford exhibits a wonderful feeling for the grandeur of land and its relation to men's endeavors that is developed to its highest expression in the use of Monument Valley.

In this first feature he uses a pass through huge cliffs that shows up in at least two other films, *The Iron Horse* and *Stagecoach.* In *Straight Shooting* the pass leads to the hideout of outlaw Black-Eyed Pete, and it is guarded by two sentinels standing on either side at the top of the steep gorge. The first time it is shown, the outlaws are riding into the pass, a long line of horses riding through with the two guards on the top like statues. In a later film this ravine will represent a pass for the transcontinental railroad that completes man's dream of bridging the continent. In this first film, the pass may not have such significant thematic relevance, but it is used to contrast man's activities with the larger structures of nature.

Ford also shows a tendency in *Straight Shooting* to photograph through doors and other framing devices. The shot of Sam riding up to the Sims farm (seen through the door of the house), jumping off his horse, and running into the house is similar to the shot in *The Searchers* that introduces Martin Pawley. The barroom doors also act constantly to frame the action. At one point Harry opens one side of the swinging door, sees his friend inside framed by the edges of the door, then walks in himself.

In later films (particularly in *The Searchers*), such visual framing takes on more developed thematic meaning, but even in *Straight Shooting* it is used expressively. When Sam overhears Flint telling Fremont to kill Harry, he is standing in the doorway of the rancher leader's house, neither inside nor out. He is acting as a farmer spy, so he has no place inside the ranchhouse.

The three-dimensionality of Ford's characters is evident in this first feature. Fremont is the killer who shoots down the farmer boy in cold blood, laughing to himself as he leaves. He even wears a moustache, the sure sign of a villain in many early American films. Before we know him as a villain, however, there is a warm, comic scene between Fremont and Harry at the bar. They meet, square off, and drink against each other. By the time they have found themselves on the roof facing each other with their guns drawn, they are so drunk that they do not know quite what to do. Each is afraid to put his gun away or to turn his back to the other, so they end up stepping back through the window, belly to belly, each with his gun against the other's. The same sort of maneuver is necessary to go downstairs. By the time they arrive back in the bar, they are fast friends again, harassing the bartender, making him "belly over the bar" to serve them, then emptying a bowl and putting it over his head.

Ford's comedy always works both as a dramatic device—in the Shakespearean sense, as counterpoint to the "tragedy" and seriousness—and to show the humanity of all the characters. Both Harry, the hero, and Fremont, the villain, are capable of getting drunk and having fun. When they walk out of the bar, Harry pulls his glove on with his teeth, since he is unable to get the other hand to work well enough.

Such a comic scene makes one little gesture in their showdown scene heartrending: After killing Fremont, Harry walks back to his horse, looking dejected. For a very short moment, he holds his horse's tail, as if needing some kind of contact after having shot a drinking buddy. It is a funny, sad little gesture, characteristic of Ford's feeling for detail.

The fight between Harry and Fremont is a classic showdown. There are first individual shots of each, then a shot of Harry's back framing Fremont in the street far in front of him. They approach each other, with Ford intercutting corresponding shots of each. As they near each other, Ford cuts to two-shot, a horse in the foreground for composition, and they pass each other, then run to either side of a building. After reaction shots of observers running to get out of the way, Ford intercuts individual shots of each behind opposite corners of the building, the shots becoming shorter and shorter. Finally, as they draw their guns, he cuts to two-shot for the shootout. As Harry walks away, Fremont lies on the ground, not just a dead villain, but a fallen friend.

The Sims family's discovery of the death of their boy Ted is another characteristic Ford scene. There is a white donkey in the stream, gently nuzzling the dead boy as he lies face down in the water. When the family comes, the donkey stands as if guarding the boy. As the father and sister embrace the dead boy, Harry is sent out to murder old Mr. Sims. As he approaches and observes them, he is shown in close-up with his hat pulled down shading his eyes, similar to a shot of Ethan in *The Searchers*. We can't be sure at this point whether he is going to kill them, but as soon as he lifts his hat it is evident his feeling is with them. There is a diffused subjective shot of him looking at the three, but unfortunately its visual quality has been lost in the one print extant of the film, and it now looks like an overexposed take. However, since Harry wipes his eyes in the cut back to him, it is fairly certain that the subjective shot was intended to show that his view of the scene was clouded by tears.

Expressionistic use of physical landscape: the pass of *Straight Shooting* and *The Iron Horse*.

Doors as framing devices.

Drinking buddies: Cheyenne Harry and Placer Fremont.

After killing his drinking buddy, Harry holds his horse's tail.

Characteristic composition: formal three-shots.

16

A person's belongings represent the person: Joan holding her brother's dinner plate.

Triangles:

Joan hopes Harry will return, but Sam comes instead.

Harry, Joan and Sam.

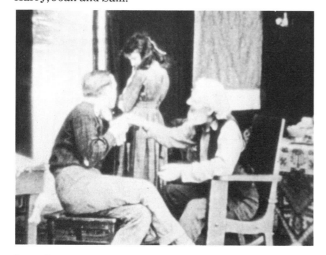

Joan, Sweetwater Sims, and Harry. The family is formed visually before it exists in the narrative.

Harry, holding his elbow in a lonesome gesture John Wayne uses at the end of *The Searchers,* ponders whether to stay with Joan and her father or leave.

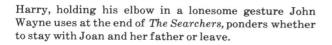

Each person—Harry, Joan, and Mr. Sims—is isolated by an oval insert in this scene after Ted's death. This device isolates the person in close-up, leaving him with his own thoughts while action carries on around him. Each feels in some way responsible for the death of the boy, and the three isolated shots serve to unite the three emotionally as an extended family, anticipating the real family they will become at the end of the film.

Ford often uses a person's belongings to stand in for the person. In *The Searchers* and *Rio Grande* a woman caresses the coat of the man she loves when she is unable to touch him. In *Straight Shooting*, Joan tenderly caresses her brother's dinner plate, breaking down and holding it like a baby. It is a lovely, tender scene, which Ford intercuts with shots of Harry alone, thinking about which side he will fight for in the battle. There is also an element of guilt in Joan's holding the plate, similar to that in *Two Rode Together*, in which a sister believes she is responsible for her brother's capture by Indians and plays his music box every night.

In the attack on the Sims ranchhouse, Ford's curious lack of expertise in maintaining constant screen direction is evident. The ranchers first assemble, line up, and ride off to attack. Then Harry goes for Black-Eyed Pete and his gang, who come riding out of their pass and down hills to the rescue. In the intercutting, screen direction (that is, constant left-to-right for the gang, right-to-left for the ranchers) is not consistent, and it is often difficult to tell which gang is which. The climactic fight is thus very confusing. In later films, Ford uses screen direction beautifully, as in the over-the-credits opening of *Rio Grande*, when he gives us a feeling of returning to the safety and comfort of the fort simply by camera direction. But this does seem to be one technique it took him a while to develop, for even as late as 1939 with *Stagecoach* (particularly in the Indian attack) he fails to maintain constant direction.

The heroes in *Straight Shooting* are the farmers, who are closer to the soil and the land than the ranchers. The rancher-versus-farmer theme is not to be repeated in Ford's Westerns, although it is one of the most often used in the Western genre. Ford did not feel this theme very personally, and in his later films ranchers and farmers were both seen as components of the force that was civilizing the West. This lesser degree of emotional involvement may have worked in favor of *Straight Shooting*, leaving Ford free to concentrate on the simple expression of the story, instead of combining it with a deeply felt theme of his own, as he did in *The Iron Horse*. His best films do combine these two, but before he gained mastery of all elements of the film-making craft, they often worked to undermine rather than enhance each other.

John Ford directing on horseback: *The Iron Horse,* 1924.

East and West meet: the historic event.

The Iron Horse is epic in conception, beginning when the transcontinental railroad is just the brain-child of a dreamer and following it through to the driving of the golden spike. John Ford likes to work within large historical events (the Revolutionary War, the life of Lincoln, the Civil War, the Indian wars, the opening of the West, the world wars), and the building of the railroad across the wilderness should have been well suited to his talents. Unfortunately, Ford does not yet seem to have the control necessary to integrate the various elements of the film. Unlike *The Horse Soldiers* in 1959, in which he isolates the necessary minor details to tell the larger story, in *The Iron Horse* Ford fails to combine successfully the delineation of the characters with the development of the larger dramatic events. The result is a very uneven, often exciting, more often ponderous epic story.

The first sequences of *The Iron Horse* charmingly combine the historical and the personal elements of the narrative. The film opens on a title card of a train with the sun rising behind it, then cuts to a snowy winter scene in the country, where Brandon and his son are talking to Marsh and his daughter. Brandon is a dreamer; he stands smoking his pipe, leaning against a tree, thinking about the transcontinental railroad. Mr. Marsh, a down-to-earth, "small" (as the title specifies) contractor, belittles Brandon for his idle dreams and calls his daughter Miriam away from him and Davy, Brandon's son, only to be chided—by none other than Abraham Lincoln—and told that someday people like him will be working for such dreamers. The titles throughout this sequence underscore the importance of the dream, telling us that the railroad will "reclaim the wilderness" and "blaze the trail." Lincoln refers to the "strong urge of progress," a "great nation pushing westward," and the "inevitable path to the West."

In this short opening sequence, all the elements of the story are set—Brandon, the dreamer, who always looks gentle and wise; Marsh, the good man who lacks vision; Davy, who admires and emulates his father; Miriam, who loves Davy. These are the personal elements. Then there are the titles, which lend the sense of history, destiny, and purpose, with Abraham Lin-

19

Davy Brandon (George O'Brien) and Corporal Casey (J. Farrell McDonald).

Davy and Miriam.

coln to tie together the personal and the historic by his physical presence and his faith in Brandon's dreams. The destinies of the two men are visually represented at the end of this sequence by their relation to Lincoln. Brandon walks away, defining a vertical line into the future, while Marsh is static under the tree beside Lincoln. If Brandon is the mover and Marsh the follower, Lincoln is the moral authority who approves the dreamer's dream.

Lincoln acts as a father to both men and their families. Ford evokes such a father figure throughout his work, often using Lincoln, even after he is long dead (*Cheyenne Autumn*). In the cavalry pictures the father figure is the commanding officer of the troop. In *Stagecoach* it is Curley, the sheriff who wants to take Ringo in for his own safety and, once that safety is no longer threatened, helps him to escape. *The Iron Horse* has one of the purest expressions of the father figure, since Lincoln has mythical connotations as father of the country.

As Davy and his father walk away from Lincoln, a very strong feeling of pioneer energy is created. They are going to bring the wilderness under their control through the railroad—a noble and worthwhile purpose. The philosophical precedents for this idea are many in the nineteenth century. The railroad represented progress, and with its completion the continent would be brought under the control of the people who could develop and use it. Its building is the first step in the taming of the wilderness; like the climbing of a mountain or the successful canoe trip down a river, the physical act of crossing the continent (and providing for others to do so) is a conquest.

The land itself is an obstacle to the dream, as well as being the source of grandeur and beauty. Brandon and Davy find a pass through which the railroad will someday be built, and at this site Brandon is killed. Brandon's death is a stopping point for the dream. Later, the railroad cannot be built beyond this spot until another dreamer (Davy) offers his help, carrying on for his father. Marsh, who is now the contractor for the railroad in the East, lacks the imagination to get past the point on his own; he would let his dishonest underlings subvert the dream if Davy had not come to his rescue.

The Indians who kill Brandon represent another physical hardship that must be overcome in taming the land. At a later point the men are working and singing when Indians come to attack them. The men stop for a moment, fight off the Indians, then go back to work, still singing. But the Indians who kill Brandon are more than simply another force to be overcome. Their leader is a white man who will later prove to be the villain. He is the only one who takes on a personal identity. Brandon sees that he is white before he dies, and Davy recognizes him in the final fight.

This conflict in meaning between the personal story

20

of Davy and the larger story of the railroad is the beginning of the film's thematic and structural problems. The Indians no longer are simply a force; the white man is the cruelest of them all (Davy watches as Bauman, disguised as an Indian, cold-bloodedly kills his father), and the missing fingers add an unnecessarily mysterious aspect to the story.

Until this point, the problem of the film was simple, carrying all the emotional impact necessary — building the railroad across America. But with the introduction of Bauman, the story of a boy's continuance of his father's dream and the grand story of crossing the continent degenerate into a good-guy bad-guy conflict, and the railroad is relegated for a time to a minor concern.

Drums Along the Mohawk has a similar structure. The characters carry the thrust of the story against the hostile forces seeking to destroy them, with a sense of inevitability that gives a mythical dimension to the story. Later in the film there is even a character similar to Bauman in the person of Caldwell, who with his eye patch is a rather melodramatic villain, but his part is so minimal that it does not overwhelm the real story, as Bauman's does in *The Iron Horse*.

In *The Iron Horse* Ford uses the "three comrades" motif, so evident in the later films, for both comedy and, in the end, tragedy. Sergeant Slattery, Corporal Casey, and Private Schultz, three close friends who fought together in the Civil War, stand at attention to greet their general when he comes to see the almost-completed railroad.

Eventually one of them is wounded, one is killed, and the last goes off with Davy to work on the other line, the Western Pacific coming toward the eastern line. When the two lines finally meet, the two remaining old friends represent the nation itself being joined as they hug each other and wish the third comrade could be there. His death stands for the hardship the whole nation has had to endure to build the railroad.

As Lincoln said, this project is as important as the war (which was raging when he signed the bill to create the line), because the needs of peace must be attended to in order to make the suffering of the war worthwhile. Slattery's death represents the sacrifice made for the railroad, a sacrifice without which the accomplishment would have less meaning in a Ford film.

Davy's father is another sacrifice to the dream, and it is a weakness of *The Iron Horse* that his death has greater significance for the mystery-crime aspects of the story than for the emotional theme of the nation struggling together for a greater good. He and Davy find the pass with no real difficulty, and then he dies for narrative reasons, not in the process of discovery or the building of the dream.

Many sequences in this film demonstrate the hardship, sacrifice, and danger of working on the line. The Indians attack the moving train at one point, and

The three comrades: Corporal Casey (J. Farrell McDonald), Sergeant Slattery (Francis Powers), and Private Schultz (James Welch), with their general.

Davy and two of his comrades.

The mobile western town follows the railroad.

when they stop it, they ride up to massacre the men. In one of Ford's most frightening images, their shadows approach and run up the side of the train. Ford often uses unusual shots to reveal attacking Indians. In the earlier scene in which Davy's father is murdered, we see first the father, who hears something, then the feet of creeping Indians. When we actually see them, it is in a shot of three of them rising up out of the night. In other films, such as *Stagecoach*, *Fort Apache*, and *Wagonmaster*, Ford pans, rather than cuts, to Indians, revealing them static, standing on a hilltop waiting to attack.

The climax of *The Iron Horse* is its weakest part, since the plot elements take over, drag out, and almost abandon the real story of the railroad. Davy fights with Jesson, is misunderstood by Miriam, and leaves for the West, providing more drama when the eastern and western parts of the railroad finally meet, but frustrating audience and plot expectations. There is a final Indian attack and then a personal fight between Bauman and Davy before the film gets on to the railroad story, when the golden spike is about to be driven. In the ceremony, Miriam and Davy stand on opposite sides of the meeting point—Miriam on the eastern and Davy on the western. Their quarrel apparently having been forgotten, each tries to get the other to cross over and join him or her, but neither will do it until the spike is in place and East and West are joined.

The final shot is of Lincoln, with the caption "His truth is marching on." His final linking with the

Sacrifice for the railroad:

The death of one of the three comrades.

The death of the saloon girl, Ruby.

railroad brings the story full circle, beginning with his endorsement of the dream and ending with its realization.

Thematically, the end of the film is right, since Davy and Miriam could not get together until the railroad did, but it is a sloppy, dragged-out conclusion to their love affair. Ford often had trouble with endings in the earlier films in his attempt to make the personal and historical stories coincide, but never is it so frustrating as in *The Iron Horse.*

Three Bad Men, like *The Iron Horse,* is about the settling of the West. "Westward the course of empire takes its way," reads one title early in the film as immigrants arrive on ships and make their way across the "trackless immensity of the West" in 1876 to seek their fortune. The immediate difference between the films is that *Three Bad Men* recognizes the dark side of that dream of empire, and the tension between the conflicting drives of "progress" keeps the film taut and underlies the personal story.

The real wealth of the land and promise of the future are in the golden grain, in the values represented by the American populist farmer, but *Three Bad Men* shows the pioneers throwing away their plows to gain speed in the rush for Indian lands and the promise of gold. The dark side of the dream of progress is represented not only by Layne Hunter and his band of outlaws, but by the good people who dream of riches. Within this structure of ambiguity, the melodramatic story of three outlaws who rescue a girl, avenge the sister of one, and lay the way for a young

The fight between Davy and Jesson.

East and West are joined.

Davy and Miriam.

John Ford in 1924.

farming family to grow up, can develop within the epic constructs of the film. Ford resolves the story with a perfect balance of personal and epic elements.

The three bad men of the title are Spade, a card shark, Mike a bank robber, and Bull, head of the trio and a horse thief. They are introduced in wanted posters, then in a long three-shot of horses at sunset. Although Bull is given a sort of justification because his sister has been wronged, there is no attempt to explain or erase the men's "outlaw" status. Ford seems fascinated with renegades, outsiders—men who do not conform to the demands of their society. From Cheyenne Harry, a reformed outlaw in *Straight Shooting*, to Tom Doniphon in *The Man Who Shot Liberty Valance*, many of Ford's heroes function outside the organization of society. And from the position of outsider, they work out a moral system that becomes in some ways more admirable than that of the society from which they cut themselves off. They are honorable men within their own code of values, like Guthrie McCabe in *Two Rode Together*, who at first seems cynical and unfeeling but turns out to be the most sensitive character in the film.

Like McCabe's mask of cynicism, the three bad men's outlaw status seems more a defense against the greed and dishonesty of the West's rough civilization than a threat to that society. In their deaths, the callous manner of the men is shown to be merely a cover-up for very sentimental natures, as they fight for the honor of dying first (Spade cheating in the draw to "win") and finally all give up their lives for the young couple. What being outlaws really means in this film is that they are outsiders, unable to do what Dan and Lee do—start a family that will settle and grow on the land.

This is most fully developed in Bull, whose most passionate interest in life is his sister. She has run off with Layne Hunter, to be shamed and finally sacrificed in a wild little town. Bull cannot help her directly; when she sees him for the first time, she is cut off from him by the frame of the window through which she gazes, and when he comes into the bar he just misses seeing her. Bull is cut off from any real emotional involvement with her and can be with her finally only when she is dying.

Bull relates to Lee in much the same removed way. She turns to him for comfort when her father is killed, not knowing that he was about to kill her before discovering she was a woman. The physical contact makes Bull uncomfortable, and when it is repeated at the camp, he decides to look for a husband for the girl. This conscious decision to withdraw from life, from a relationship with a woman, is at the heart of what makes Bull an outlaw and later, in *The Searchers*, what makes Ethan Edwards an outsider. It is an expression of something deep within himself that cuts him off from contact with other people and prevents him from coming to terms with life.

Three Bad Men, 1926.

Foreground action against background panorama: Dan O'Malley heads West.

The first views of the three bad men: both mythical representations.

The three outlaws watch the endless march of pioneers.

Spade, the first to die.

Mike, the second to die, and Bull, the last to die for Lee.

Dan, the young Irishman whom Bull chooses for Lee, lacks this "outsider" dimension and, at the same time, lacks a certain depth that Ford's outsiders always have. The root of that condition just outside society seems to be repressed sexuality, which separates Bull from both his sister and Lee. Dan has a very open and direct sexuality, flirting with Lee when he first sees her and nearly kissing her a few moments later. Thus, Bull is a precursor to Ford's most sophisticated and complex heroes, Ethan Edwards, Spig Weed, and Tom Doniphon, in that repressed sexuality separates him from any real interaction with emotional values in life, yet at the same time gives him a yearning, unfinished quality that is enormously attractive. The viewer can relate his own feelings of incompleteness to the character, who works out the lack in his life in a stylized, ritualistic form of sacrifice.

Visually, the film is not as rich as later ones, but again, as with *Straight Shooting*, there are many indications of Ford's later brilliance. Framing devices are perhaps the most evident in *Three Bad Men*. Ford frames Dan and Lee through a huge wagon wheel when they first meet, and he later uses the frames of the window to cut Bull off from his sister. In one very beautiful shot the pioneer wagon train is filmed through the arch of a wagon, with a mother and her child just inside the arch. This is very expressive of Ford's dream of progress: mother and child representing young families as the westward movement of the train shows the drive for the completion of the dream. Layne and Bull's sister Millie are framed by a little window when they talk to each other. Millie tells Layne there is a minister in town who can marry them, and Layne laughs at her, closing the sliding door to the little window and shutting her out physically and emotionally.

The rescue of the women from Layne's men at the church, à la *Birth of a Nation,* is the weakest part of the film, with only the intercutting of Millie and Bull adding real interest to the story's development. The action is not very well handled. As in *Straight Shooting,* Ford does not control screen direction correctly, and the audience becomes confused over which riders are Layne's men and which are the decent people of the community coming to rescue the women and children. The reaction shots of crying babies and frightened women may be reminiscent of Griffith, but they are not very meaningful in this film's terms.

In their last scene, Lee kisses Bull goodbye, knowing he is going to die for her. The relation between the noble idea of sacrifice for the little family-to-be and the very overt sexual content of the Lee-Bull relationship gives the sentiment its depth; it has a deeply personal content as well as an uplifting, societal content. The interaction and perfect junction of the two creates the great emotional power of *Three Bad Men.*

Framing to show isolation: Bull's sister Millie.

The dream of westward expansion.

Lee and Bull: repressed sexuality.

Formal composition of ritual: Millie's death and funeral.

Lee and Dan: unrepressed sexuality.

The three bad men continue to watch over their charges.

The young farming family: Dan, Lee, and their baby.

Mike, Bull, and Spade.

3
STAGECOACH

CREDITS

Production company, Walter Wanger Productions. *Director,* John Ford. *Producer,* John Ford. *Executive producer,* Walter Wanger. *Script,* Dudley Nichols; based on Ernest Haycox's story "STAGE TO LORDSBURG." *Director of photography,* Bert Glennon. *Special effects,* Ray Binger. *Music,* Richard Hageman, W. Franke Harling, John Leipold, Leo Shuken, Louis Gruenberg, adapted from seventeen American folk tunes of the early 1880s. *Arranger and conductor,* Boris Morros. *Editorial supervisor,* Otho Lovering. *Editors,* Dorothy Spencer, Walter Reynolds. *Art director,* Alexander Toluboff. *Set decorator,* Wiard B. Ihnen. *Costumes,* Walter Plunkett. *Assistant director,* Wingate Smith. *Second unit director,* Yakima Canutt. *Locations filmed in Kernville, Dry Lake, Victorville, Fremont Pass, Calabasas, and Chatsworth, California, Kayenta and Mesa, Arizona, and Monument Valley, Utah. Released March 2, 1939. Running time,* 97 minutes. *Distributor,* United Artists.

CAST

John Wayne *(the Ringo Kid)*, Claire Trevor *(Dallas)*, John Carradine *(Hatfield)*, Thomas Mitchell *(Dr. Josiah Boone)*, Andy Devine *(Buck)*, Donald Meek *(Samuel Peacock)*, Louise Platt *(Lucy Mallory)*, Tim Holt *(Lieutenant Blanchard)*, George Bancroft *(Sheriff Curly Wilcox)*, Berton Churchill *(Henry Gatewood)*, Tom Tyler *(Hank Plummer)*, Chris Pin Martin *(Chris)*, Elvira Rios *(Yakima, his wife)*, Francis Ford *(Billy Pickett)*, Marga Daighton *(Mrs. Pickett)*, Kent Odell *(Billy Pickett, Jr.)*, Yakima Canutt *(white scout)*, Chief Big Tree *(Indian scout)*, Harry Tenbrook *(telegraph operator)*, Jack Pennick *(Jerry, the bartender)*, Paul McVey *(Wells Fargo agent)*, Cornelius Keefe *(Captain Whitney)*, Florence Lake *(Mrs. Nancy Whitney)*, Louis Mason *(sheriff)*, Brenda Fowler *(Mrs. Gatewood)*, Walter McGrail *(Captain Sickels)*, Joseph Rickson *(Luke Plummer)*, Vester Pegg *(Ike Plummer)*, William Hoffer *(sergeant)*, Bryant Washburn *(Captain Simmons)*, Nora Cecil *(Dr. Boone's housekeeper)*, Helen Gibson, Dorothy Appleby *(saloon girls)*, Buddy Roosevelt, Bill Cody *(ranchers)*, Chief White Horse *(Indian chief)*, Duke Lee *(sheriff of Lordsburg)*, Mary Kathleen Walker *(Lucy's baby)*, Ed Brady, Steve Clemente, Theodore Larch, Fritzi Brunette, Leonard Trainor, Chris Phillips, Tex Driscoll, Teddy Billings, John Eckert, Al Lee, Jack Mohr, Patsy Doyle, Wiggie Blowne, Margaret Smith.

Although there is evidence of Indian trouble between Tonto and Lordsburg, eight people (joined by a ninth on the trail), each with his own reason, take the stage to Lordsburg. Lucy Mallory, going to join her husband, is pregnant and has her baby in a way station halfway there. Drunken Doc Boone delivers it successfully, and the outcast Dallas and outlaw Ringo fall in love. Indians attack the stagecoach on the final day of the journey. Hatfield is killed, Peacock is wounded, and the cavalry comes to the rescue in an exciting action sequence. In Lordsburg, Ringo kills the Plummer brothers, who victimized his family, and he and Dallas are sent off across the border to his ranch by Doc Boone and Curly, the sheriff.

*S*tagecoach is John Ford's most famous Western, possibly his most famous film. André Bazin called it the classic Western, and it is often regarded as the standard against which others of the genre are measured. But when placed within the context of Ford's body of work and judged by that high standard, the film does not measure up to its critical reputation.

In *Stagecoach* many of Ford's themes can be found, but they are superficially stated and lack the rich complexity necessary for them to become meaningful outside the context of the narrative. The film is a classic parable of a "journey into hell"—the hero (in this case the group) must undertake a journey that brings him face to face with mirror images of his own weaknesses and flaws, but in the form of powerful obstacles for him to overcome before he can pass through his hell and emerge, cleansed and reborn, into the light. In mythology the setting is often a real hell, an underworld through which a hero must pass to prove himself. The descent and ascent are actual, whereas in later literature they are symbolic. The function of the myth remains the same—to affirm the value of life in the face of its own weaknesses, which lead inevitably to death.

In *Stagecoach*, the goal is group interaction, which affirms the group over the pettiness of the individuals. This robs the myth of its most powerful ingredient, the wholeness and individuality of the hero, because in *Stagecoach* each character is merely a part of the whole being that is the group. Their dangers are self-created (as in Ford's greater works, a reflection of the characters' inner torments) but are group expressed; that is, they are group tensions, which are alleviated when the group becomes united as the pretenses and protections of the town are stripped away.

The problem with this kind of morality play in the *oeuvre* of a deeply personal director is that it does not leave him the freedom he needs to develop his themes of ambiguity and conflicting drives, with which the individual must come to terms. As a consequence,

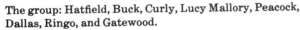

The group: Hatfield, Buck, Curly, Lucy Mallory, Peacock, Dallas, Ringo, and Gatewood.

Ford's richly suggestive visual style can be no more than another morally clear element in a very neat structure of social values, and this is less than the highest use of his talents. The resulting film is fine by almost any standards except perhaps those of Ford's own work.

The dramatic contrivance characteristic of *Stagecoach* is rigidly based on the A-B structural scheme —scenes of action alternating with scenes of character interaction until four scenes of each have been played out. The four scenes of character interaction are first, the town of Tonto, second, the way station where the stagecoach stops for food, third, the Mexican outpost where the baby is born, and last, the town of Lordsburg. The action sequences are first, the cavalry and the telegraph wires, then the first leg of the trip to Lordsburg, then the second leg in the snow, and last, the run to Lordsburg with the Indians attacking and the cavalry rescuing. In these action sequences there is a good deal of cutting to inside the stagecoach, where character development goes on, and in Lordsburg there is the gunfight, but these do not serve to integrate the two elements. In the case of the cutting between the stagecoach moving through Monument Valley and the people inside it, it becomes very apparent and somewhat distracting that these two diverse dramatic elements are being counterpointed.

There are nine major characters in the film—Buck, the stage driver; Curly, the marshal; Gatewood, the banker; Peacock, the whiskey drummer; Hatfield, the gambler; Lucy Mallory, the pregnant wife; Doc Boone, the drunken doctor; Dallas, the "good bad girl"; and Ringo, the escaped convict. Each of them is closer to a theater piece than to a real character. It is not that they are one-dimensional (only the banker is never given an opportunity to show a good side), but that they fit with such contrived perfection into the script. Each has his place that helps make up the whole of *Stagecoach*. The impression is that they are thrown together in this crisis according to some higher plan (the scriptwriter's), and each is included because of some special attribute or lack therof that permits him a place in the drama. Through contact with the others, each character is revealed, and through his part, each helps reveal the others.

Of course, such contrivance must be present to an extent in any film or play, but where it becomes so orchestrated that the characters no longer live except as part of the carefully balanced whole, the result is a theater piece that can perhaps be admired but that does not have an organic energy of its own. Everything we know about each character we know for a reason, and the reason exists only for the purpose of the whole script. There is little mysterious, ambiguous, complex, or intriguing about any of the characters— each exists primarily as a foil for the others.

Buck is the only comic character who never goes beyond that role, except perhaps in the scene in which

News of Geronimo comes before the telegraph wires are cut.

he holds the baby and says, "Doggone" over and over (as Henry Fonda does in *Drums Along the Mohawk* when his baby is born). He is the stupid one, for whom things must be explained so that plot elements may be revealed to the audience. Buck is a caricature from beginning to end. His form and voice are the first things we know about him. They are comic and incongruous, as are the elements of his life that we learn. He has a Mexican wife with a hundred relatives, so that poor Buck has nothing but beans to eat when he goes home. He is also a coward, but not one to be taken seriously. He is never given an opportunity to talk in the discussion sessions they hold to decide what they will do next, and unlike Peacock, he is not taken seriously even when he is wounded.

Gatewood, the banker, is the "bad" character who constantly reminds us how human the others are. He is seen first with the women who run Dallas out of town, then in his bank with the shadow of a cross behind him like a curse. He is given some slight justification for his bad character in the form of a shrewish wife, whose invitation of the priggish women of the town to lunch is the last straw, causing him to decide to run away with the bank's money. He is overbearing to the cavalry, demanding their protection and giving them orders, and he rails against the government, bank examiners, taxes, and the other people on the stagecoach. He is as insensitive as the politician in *The Horse Soldiers,* seeing everything from his selfish point of view. He yells at poor, dumb Buck for sleeping on his money bags, and he is finally caught in the middle of his self-righteous indignation when demanding that Ringo be handcuffed upon their arrival in Lordsburg.

No matter how satisfying it is to see the cowardly old hypocrite exposed, our satisfaction is mitigated by the fact that he has never been allowed a moment of humanity. He wants to move on, regardless of Lucy Mallory's health, he abuses good old Doc Boone, who has come through for the baby, and he finally tries to persecute Ringo, who has been more responsible than anyone else for their survival. This melodramatic kind of villain adds nothing to the film and makes us suspect the emotions we feel for the rest of the company.

Peacock functions both as comic relief and as an appealing figure in need of protection. When we first see him at the end of the bar, as Doc comes in for a drink in Tonto, Peacock is the apex of a triangle formed by the bartender, Doc, and himself. Thus, he is the focus of the conversation between Doc and the bartender. When Doc learns Peacock's profession, he moves up to him and physically and psychologically takes him over by an arm around his shoulder and a counterfeit offer of friendship contingent upon the salesman's samples. Later, in the stagecoach, Doc carefully wipes Peacock's eyes and pats his arm while finishing off another sample bottle.

Peacock is a coward, but he has a good little heart, and he thinks first about the newborn baby. This humanity makes it very poignant when he is wounded in the Indian attack. Although no one can remember his name, Dallas speaks to him when they arrive in Lordsburg, and he functions throughout as a minor (in personality, ability, courage, force, and influence) but kindly character whose main purpose is comic foil for the larger character of Doc. And like Gatewood, he is also Eastern, which counterpoints the Westernness of the rest of the company, particularly Ringo, who has the ease, graciousness, courage, and lack of pretense or preconceptions of the Westerner.

Curly represents the humane law, a fatherly kind of authority. He wants to take Ringo back to prison to save him from certain death, although he admits to Buck that the reward would do him good. He always speaks for the good of them all, and he is the peacemaker in the feud between Doc and Gatewood. His lack of emotion or passion keeps him from being a very appealing character, but it is his role in the whole unity of the company to be authoritative and distant, a steady structure against which the hysteria of Doc, Gatewood, Hatfield, and Buck can be measured.

Hatfield is the most dramatic. He is the fallen aristocrat, the gambler with superficial Eastern sensibilities and a past that might be interesting if it did not serve so neat a purpose in the extent to which we know it. He offers the character of Lucy Mallory the only status to which she can relate, although he has become a gunman and gambler since he served with her father in the Civil War. He would have more humanity if he had less assumed dignity. His attentions to Lucy Mallory slight Dallas, and the inadvertent sacrifice of his life for Lucy becomes

simply a theatrical gesture as we see his gun (held at Lucy's head, with its last bullet in the chamber to save her from a "fate worse than death") fall from his hand to signal his death. His Eastern insistence on form as opposed to content (portrayed by the other characters) reduces him to a caricature, which is underscored by his melodramatic clothes. Hatfield functions as a foil for Lucy Mallory and little more; he is simply a force by which to show the difference between Lucy and Dallas, which the film proves to be arbitrary and incorrect.

Doc Boone is the prototype for Ford's drunken-doctor character, which appears in other films and is most developed as Doc Holliday in *My Darling Clementine.* He begins as a kindly drunk, a fellow to Dallas, both victims of a disease called "social prejudice." His antics with Peacock are charming, especially his solicitousness with regard to the little man's health and comfort when he wraps the scarf around Peacock's neck and wipes his eyes. Doc reaches a high point of comedy in the first way station, where he cavorts with Francis Ford, who breaks up over his antics. They drink together as the others work out their social status with regard to seating at the table, providing a counterpoint for the tensions in the rest of the company.

Doc reaches his lowest point just before the baby is born, when he is dead drunk when most needed. He rises to his professional calling and puts himself through torture to be a fit doctor. When he successfully delivers the baby, he takes a well-deserved drink in a scene to be repeated in *My Darling Clementine* after Doc Holliday has performed an operation.

Doctors in films and in our society take on larger-than-life dimensions because of their powers of life and death. To be human as well, their weaknesses must be similarly exaggerated. Ford uses the drunken doctor over and over, but it is in *Stagecoach* and *My Darling Clementine* that they play the largest roles. Doc Boone does not have the darker implications that color Doc Holliday, so he becomes the most lovable character in the film. It is to Doc that Dallas goes when she is agonizing over her decision to marry Ringo, and to Doc that Ringo goes to discuss the problem. He is father figure to both of them without being an authority figure like Curly, and it is schematically right that Doc and Curly send them on their way when they leave together for Ringo's ranch across the border.

Ringo is perfect—he has all the good qualities of honor, ability, ease, grace, gentleness, and the ability to love without regard for social form. We first see the Ringo Kid standing by the side of the road, and Ford rapidly tracks in on his face. He appears like a god out of the desert. John Wayne immediately registers his star quality in the close-up, and we are drawn to him irresistibly. Without Wayne's powerful presence, the character of Ringo would not carry us; it is too "good"

Dallas, Gatewood, and Lucy Mallory.

The Ringo Kid: like a god out of the desert.

and too overexplained. Ringo was in jail for defending his family against the no-good Plummers, and he escaped to avenge their deaths. Lines like "There are some things a man just can't run away from" are clichés today, but not when John Wayne speaks them. There is no question that he will defeat the Plummer brothers—Hank Plummer holds a "dead man's hand" in the poker game he is playing when the stage rolls into Lordsburg.

There is a feeling of destiny about the gunfight, created by high camera angles and by dark shadows on the three Plummers, which seem to entrap and doom them. This feeling is actualized in the shot in which Ringo throws himself to the ground and kills them all. The success of *Stagecoach* seems largely a result of this casting. No other actor could bring to the Ringo character the necessary mythical purposefulness required to lead the journey to Lordsburg against all odds.

Dallas is the prostitute with the heart of gold. Her questionable past is explained by the fact that she lost her parents very early and had to make it on her own in a country that provided nothing for a pretty, single

The stagecoach arrives at the first way station.

The social structure: Lucy and Dallas, with Hatfield approving.

Dallas and Ringo.

woman to do but work in saloons. She is not only without stain because of her past, she is enhanced by having gone through it and emerged without scars. She is reminiscent of Lillian Gish in *Way Down East*, who is given an added element of tragedy and depth of character by having been tricked into bearing a child. Both she and Dallas remain essentially innocent in the face of corruption. Dallas was forced into a socially condemned role, but from the very first moment our sympathies are with her as the sour, pinched-faced old matrons of the town drive her out. She is dressed in gay, graceful tones, while they are somber and stiff. Dallas's humility is proof of her worth; she, more than anyone else, believes that she is not as good as Lucy Mallory, not fit to be a decent man's wife. Her acceptance of her role and Ringo's defense of it make her seem all the more appealing.

Stagecoach is for most people the archetypal Western; yet in many ways it runs exactly counter to the expectations of the genre, most evidently in the presentation of its women. Dallas is the questionable girl who, according to convention, should be dark-haired and kindly and should eventually die or in some less radical way give up the hero. In *Stagecoach*, not only is Dallas the blonde, truly innocent woman, but she gets the hero. Lucy, the refined Eastern woman, has dark hair and is finally shown to be shallow and undeserving of Dallas's concern. Their goodbye in Lordsburg, when Lucy starts to say, "If there is ever anything I can do for you," and realizes that Dallas said almost exactly the same thing to her earlier and was rebuffed, is an affirmation of the values represented by Dallas as opposed to those of Lucy.

The musical score of *Stagecoach* is notable. Ford uses music beautifully as a rule rather than an

36

exception. He introduces the town of Tonto to the boisterous strains of "Bury Me Not on the Lone Prairie" as the stage pulls in, and that song becomes the stagecoach theme as it crosses the desert to Lordsburg. In Tonto, Doc and Dallas march to the stage in time to a marching version of the theme, which provides both comic counterpoint and a fare-well theme for the fugitives.

"I Dream of Jeannie" is Lucy Mallory's theme, heard when we first see her and often thereafter. The most powerful use of this theme is when Hatfield is about to kill her to save her from the Indians and she is crying and praying at the same time. The theme comes in quietly, rises as Hatfield's gun falls away, and is gradually overpowered by the cavalry "charge." The introduction of the cavalry is by the music and has a very powerful emotional effect—we hear them before ever seeing them.

Stagecoach marks Ford's first use of Monument Valley, and although its character is not as fully developed as in later Westerns, it functions well to isolate and enclose the world of the film. Monument Valley is a larger-than-life backdrop against which the struggles of men take on a larger meaning. It is mainly the use of the valley that gives *Stagecoach* its mythical implications of a journey into an inferno where men's determination not only brings them through, but creates new life so that the whole of the company emerges from the journey reborn. The unchangeable monuments in the background are eternal, untouched by men and their battles, yet moved by their transcendent purposes. If the desert of the valley is seen as another obstacle put in their path by the forces of nature, then their achievement is even more meaningful on the grander scale of man against his environment.

More in keeping with Ford's themes, however, the valley seems to be symbolic of the forces of nature, which offer man neither aid nor obstacle but are only a stage upon which he can work out his dreams. Monument Valley is perfect as such a stage; it is self-

Victims of a disease called "social prejudice."

contained and self-limiting, and within it an enclosed worldview is not only possible, but necessary. Within it life (and the living of it) must be created through the efforts of man—the environment does not do it for them. The birth of the baby then takes on mythical significance—life created within such a world is a symbol of the energy, perseverance, and endurance of man himself. It took the whole of the company to create the life, and it took Monument Valley to require that affirmation.

The journey to Lordsburg has the feeling of destiny; with its accomplishment each character will have faced his fate. Lucy has her baby, loses her husband, and acknowledges higher values than those learned by social training. Dallas proves herself more valuable and meaningful than she had ever thought she was. Doc proves his worth to himself and everyone else by rising to his professional expectations and then going on to save Dallas and Ringo from "the blessings of civilization." Hatfield meets his "tragic" melodramatic death just as he would have killed Lucy Mallory in his last chivalrous act. Peacock faces his own cowardice and comes out wounded but intact.

The stagecoach crosses snow-covered Monument Valley.

The stagecoach with its cavalry escort.

Gatewood reaches his reward in Lordsburg. Buck and Curly, as the most tangential, functional characters, are essentially unchanged by the experience. All comes together like a mathematical equation. And it is precisely this complete lack of ambiguity in the work of such a profoundly ambiguous artist that leaves the film satisfying in a shallow rather than a deeply emotional way.

The next morning: Lucy, Doc Boone, and Dallas.

The impending birth: Hatfield, Lucy Mallory, and Curly.

Life created in crisis: the new baby.

Dallas and Doc Boone.

Ringo and Dallas.

Lucy Mallory and Hatfield.

News of the Indians.

A chivalrous act: Hatfield and a murdered woman.

The Indians attack.

Crossing the river.

Ringo defending the stagecoach.

40

Lordsburg.

John Ford and the company on the set of *Stagecoach*.

4
DRUMS ALONG THE

CREDITS

Production company, 20th Century–Fox. *Director,* John Ford. *Producer,* Raymond Griffith. *Executive producer,* Darryl F. Zanuck. *Script,* Lamar Trotti, Sonya Levien; based on Walter D. Edmonds' novel. *Directors of photography,* Bert Glennon, Ray Rennahan. *Color process,* Three-Color Technicolor. *Color consultants,* Natalie Kalmus, Henry Jaffa. *Music,* Alfred Newman. *Editor,* Robert Simpson. *Sound-effects editor,* Robert Parrish. *Art directors,* Richard Day, Mark Lee Kirk. *Set decorator,* Thomas Little. *Costumes,* Gwen Wakeling. *Released November 3, 1939. Running time,* 103 minutes. *Certain shots and sequences were later used in* BUFFALO BILL *(Fox, 1944) and* MOHAWK *(Fox, 1956). Distributor,* 20th Century–Fox.

CAST

Claudette Colbert *(Lana Borst Martin),* Henry Fonda *(Gilbert Martin),* Edna May Oliver *(Mrs. McKlennan),* Eddie Collins *(Christian Reall),* John Carradine *(Caldwell),* Dorris Bowdon *(Mary Reall),* Jessie Ralph *(Mrs. Weaver),* Arthur Shields *(Father Rosenkranz),* Robert Lowery *(John Weaver),* Roger Imof *(General Nicholas Herkimer),* Francis Ford *(Joe Boleo),* Ward Bond *(Adam Hartmann),* Kay Linaker *(Mrs. Demooth),* Russell Simpson *(Dr. Petry),* Chief Big Tree *(Blue Back),* Spencer Charters *(Fisn, innkeeper),* Arthur Aysleworth *(George),* Si Jenks *(Jacobs),* Jack Pennick *(Amos),* Charles Tannen *(Robert Johnson),* Paul McVey *(Captain Mark Demooth),* Elizabeth Jones *(Mrs. Reall),* Lionel Pape *(general),* Clarence Wilson *(paymaster),* Edwin Maxwell *(pastor),* Clara Blandick *(Mrs. Borst),* Beulah Hall Jones *(Daisy),* Robert Greig *(Mr. Borst).*

SYNOPSIS:

Just before the Revolutionary War, Gil Martin marries Lana, an Eastern girl, and brings her to his cabin and farm in the Mohawk Valley. She is first terrified by Blue Back but soon becomes a farm wife. The English are stirring up the Indians, and Gil and Lana's farm is burned to the ground in an Indian attack. Lana also loses her baby, leaving them to face the winter without hope or future. Mrs. McKlennan takes them in as hired help, and they work her farm.

MOHAWK

Gil goes to war, and only Lana's persistence, refusing to believe he is dead and dragging him out of the mud, brings him home again. She is pregnant again, and with the birth of their baby they are totally happy.

Another Indian attack comes, and the community goes to the fort, which is almost overrun before Gil returns with reinforcements. The farmers win the day and hoist their new flag over the fort.

I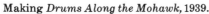n many of the traditional respects *Drums Along the Mohawk* is not a Western at all; it does not use horses except as farm animals, and it is set in the Mohawk Valley. The time period — that of the Revolutionary War — predates considerably the post-Civil War period we associate with the Western. In more basic, important ways, however, *Drums Along the Mohawk* is definitely a Western and even more definitely a John Ford Western. Many of his ideas about white civilization and its mission in the West have their purest expression in this film.

Gil Martin is the yeoman farmer who plays so large a part in agrarian-populist mythology. He built his own home, to which he brings his new bride, and they both work to raise a family there and *individually* to protect it from any outside forces. When there is talk of political parties in the film, it is "the American" party that counts, and all that really means is that the white farmers have the right to do what they want with their land.

These farmers are gentle, good-natured men who want nothing more than to be allowed to farm but who are capable of asserting that right by force when necessary. Even the minister is capable of force when what he believes in is threatened, and he calls the Christian God down upon the heads of his enemies.

These forces of religion, mission, and politics combine in *Drums Along the Mohawk* to create a power incapable of being defeated. The preacher says in the same breath, "Trust in the Lord and don't shoot until you can make every shot count." When he kills a man, he asks that "God have mercy on his soul," then observes, "I must be shooting a little to the left." He asks the Lord to notice that they are low on ammunition, and his only qualm about killing comes when he is forced to put Joe, a white man, out of his increasing misery.

There is no doubt of rightness here — God is on their side, and they will win because of it. Their mission is to farm the land, and any force that dares interrupt it will know the wrath of their Lord. The Indians in this film are emissaries of that force, and fire is its symbol. The Indians use fire to burn the wheat, the house, and all the things that Lana brought so carefully from her Eastern home. Later they use fire to kill Joe and to attack the fort.

The most impressive scene, however, is in Mrs. McKlennan's bedroom when the Indians come in to burn the house down. The old woman, through the force of her rightness, her absolute certainty that they are Savage and she is Civilized, forces them to carry her bed downstairs. That bed is the symbol of her life with her husband. It stands for her civilization, against which their savagery has no chance, even though they are two strong Indians and she is one old woman. She dies shortly afterward, through an accident with no real reason or rationale except that

Making *Drums Along the Mohawk,* 1939.

Agents of chaos and destruction: Indians and fire.

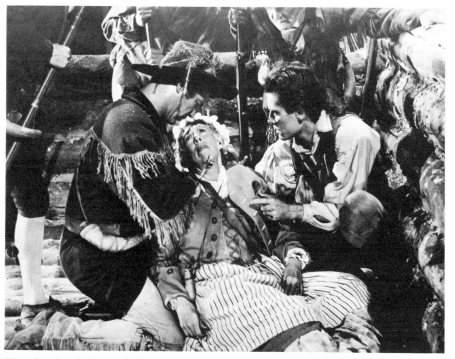

The death of Mrs. McKlennan: an accident with no rationale except that her bed and her home are gone, and she has no strength without them.

The minister: preacher and fighter.

The eastern wedding.

her bed and her home are gone, and she has no strength without them.

The different values of East and West are seen in the character of Lana. The film opens on her wedding bouquet, then pulls back to reveal the wedding and all the well-dressed men and women who attend it. The colors are rich and artificial, as is her dress when they set out in their wagon. The house she is leaving is large and Eastern, and Gil never quite seems to fit in to it. Lana makes a little face when Gil mentions the cow they will take with them. As they progress, Gil seems to fit better and better into the landscape, and Lana becomes more and more out of place. She gets dirty, and upon arriving at the cabin is wet and tired, a mess in her finery. She becomes hysterical at the sight of Blue Back, the Christian Indian, and must be slapped out of it.

From this low point we go to a beautiful sunny day in which she and Gil are gathering hay and playing, completely happy. When they must leave their home during the Indian attack, she wants to take the cow, an indication of how far she has come in her shift of values and capabilities. She makes the final step from Eastern girl to frontier woman when she shoots an Indian in the attack on the fort; the captain's wife is still sniveling helplessly as Lana was at first, but Lana has given up her possessions, her pretenses, and finally her weaknesses.

The captain's wife is a contrast for one side of Lana —the Eastern side that needs nice furniture and equates value with rank. A constant example of a woman who will not adjust, the captain's wife keeps reminding the other woman that her husband is the captain, that her Eastern home was fine and rich, and that she is small and petty in her jealousy of Lana. If she and the captain have children (a sure sign of fertility in all aspects of life on the frontier farm), we never see them.

The contrast on the other side is Mrs. McKlennan, a complete frontier woman. She has no glamour, no pretense about her, and we love her from the very first scene. She is kind, capable, strong, and faithful to her husband in every way, even to understanding his masculine joy in fighting. She has a clear idea of her place in the frontier, and she seeks neither to embroider it with fancy clothes and furniture nor to expand it by doing men's work.

The birth of Lana's baby is one of the purest expressions of the frontier woman's value. When Lana is first said to be expecting, she becomes an object of affection and the center of attention. A woman's prime duty on the frontier is to bear children, preferably male children. She loses that baby because of the Indians and the fire, leaving Gil and Lana completely stripped of everything they had a day before—home, crops, family. When she tells him she is going to have another, he is near death himself after the battle, and this offer of life is her gift to him. She says that she feels as though she is beginning to live again.

A beautiful Fordian touch is that for Lana's baby to be born, the general must die. The juxtaposition of her announcing the birth and his death from an operation indicates that the two events are related, just as her bringing Gil back from the dead is related to the general's death. It is as though he gives up his life that the young might continue to live and be born, according to a nature-determined order of things.

Ford makes full use of weather symbolism in *Drums Along the Mohawk*. The film opens on a beautiful day when Gil and Lana are married, and night falls as they stop at an inn. With the darkness comes Caldwell, the English sympathizer who masterminds the destruction of the farms. Their arrival at their cabin, a low point for Lana, is in the midst of a violent storm. She sees Blue Back against a sky of hostility, and her panic is reflected in the elements. They gather hay happily in the bright sunshine, then return to their burned-out cabin in the dreary cold winter. Gil comes back home from the battle in a storm; the wounded and dying seem a reflection of the weather. Finally, the Indians attack the fort at night, the dark acting as a cover for their advance. As Gil runs away from them, we see the sun coming up, and by the time it is fully day, he has outdistanced them. It is as though they lack power in the daylight.

Although Gil and Lana are the focus of the story, there is a very strong feeling for the community in the film. When they first go to the fort, the community center of the area, they walk among friends and neighbors, cutting a swath, with Lana in her pink dress and bonnet. The women bustle around her, and the men drill for their ladies, joking and playing all the while.

In all Ford's films, the community reaches its full expression only after it has won hard-fought battles, and this is the case in the last scene of *Drums Along the Mohawk*. Gil and Lana walk out toward the gate in a tracking shot that stops when the American flag comes into frame. They gaze at their flag and all it represents, as it is hoisted on the church (and fort) steeple. There are low-angle shots of Gil and Lana, the black woman who worked for Mrs. McKlennan, the Indian Blue Back, and others, as they look up at their flag. Here is summed up all they have been fighting for: their community center—the fort and the church.

There is no doubt or ambiguity in this film—the American dream is still very much intact. This is possibly the only Ford film that deals so explicitly with the American dream where everything comes together with no uncertain edges. There are no questions or regrets at the end of the film. Perhaps there is a hint of the cost of what they have won as the parson sits staring off into space, muttering, "I

Caldwell: a threat to the newlyweds and the new country.

Lana and Blue Back, the Christian Indian.

Taming the land: the yeoman farmer.

Fleeing the Indians: leaving their home behind.

The war from Lana's point of view: watching and waiting.

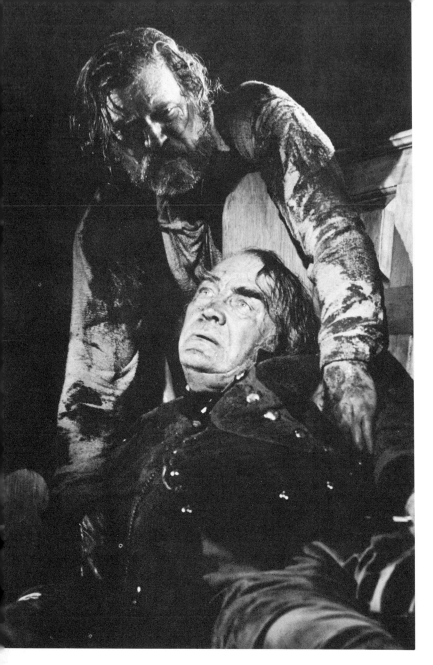

killed a man." But this is mitigated by his earlier role as a militant clergyman and seems more a superficial, passing concern than a real question into the validity of what he has done.

The combination of religious, military, and agrarian values gives the film a validity that cannot be questioned. The Western yeoman cannot be stopped; he has God and nature on his side. Tilling the soil for the greater good of America (that is, mankind), putting away artificial Eastern values for purer, more natural ones, and winning his battle with the forces of darkness and evil, the yeoman farmer has no room for question or doubt. He knows he is right, and at this point in his career, so does Ford.

Death of the general: sacrifice for the new country and the new family.

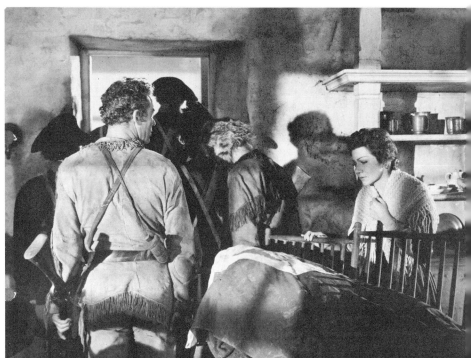

The birth of Gil and Lana's baby.

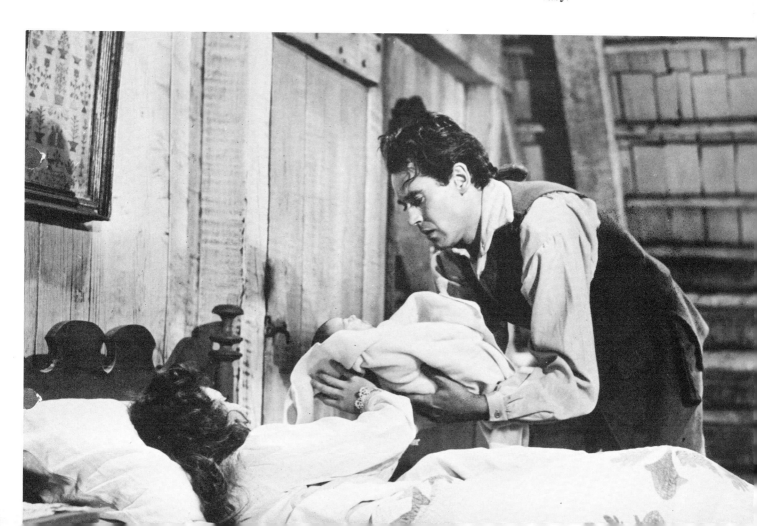

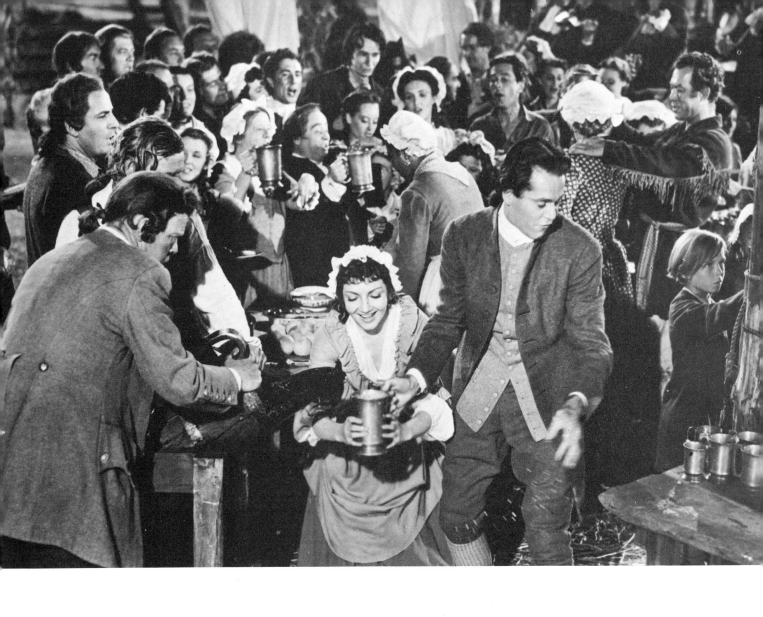

The community having a
dance.

54

The battle for the fort: Gil going for help.

The sentry guarding the fort.

Lana and her child.

After the battle:

Blue Back with Caldwell's
eyepatch.

The triumph of white civilization in the wilderness.

5
MY DARLING CLEMENTINE

CREDITS

Production company, 20th Century-Fox. *Director,* John Ford. *Producer,* Samuel G. Engel. *Script,* Samuel G. Engel, Winston Miller. *Story,* Sam Hellman; based on Stuart N. Lake's novel WYATT EARP, FRONTIER MARSHAL. *Director of photography,* Joseph P. MacDonald. *Special effects,* Fred Sersen. *Music,* Cyril J. Mockridge. *Conductor,* Edward B. Powell. *Editor,* Dorothy Spencer. *Art directors,* James Basevi, Lyle R. Wheeler. *Set decorators,* Thomas Little, Fred J. Rode. *Costumes,* René Hubert. *Assistant director* William Eckhardt. *Locations filmed in Kayenta, Arizona, and Monument Valley, Utah. Released December 3, 1946. Running time,* 97 minutes. *Second remake of* FRONTIER MARSHAL *(Fox, 1934, Fox, 1939). Distributor,* 20th Century-Fox.

CAST

Henry Fonda *(Wyatt Earp),* Linda Darnell *(Chihuahua),* Victor Mature *(Dr. John "Doc" Holliday),* Walter Brennan *(Old Man Clanton),* Tim Holt *(Virgil Earp),* Ward Bond *(Morgan Earp),* Cathy Downs *(Clementine Carter),* Alan Mowbray *(Granville Thorndyke),* John Ireland *(Billy Clanton),* Grant Withers *(Ike Clanton),* Roy Roberts *(mayor),* Jane Darwell *(Kate Nelson),* Russell Simpson *(John Simpson),* Francis Ford *(Dad, old soldier),* J. Farrell McDonald *(Mac, barman),* Don Garner *(James Earp),* Ben Hall *(barber),* Arthur Walsh *(hotel clerk),* Jack Pennick *(coach driver),* Louis Mercier *(François),* Mickey Simpson *(Sam Clanton),* Fred Libby *(Phin Clanton),* Harry Woods *(Luke),* Charles Stevens *(Indian Joe).*

SYNOPSIS:

As Wyatt Earp and his three brothers drive their cattle west from Texas, they come to the wild town of Tombstone. Leaving James, the youngest, to guard the cattle, they ride into town to get a shave and find the town "wide open" and dangerous. Wyatt subdues a drunken Indian and gets an offer to be marshal of the town. He refuses but then accepts after returning to the camp, to find his herd stolen and his brother murdered.

Wyatt meets Doc Holliday, the "real power of the town," in Doc's saloon, and after challenging one another to a stale-

Wyatt Earp.

mate, the two become friends. Clementine Carter, an Eastern girl who was Doc's nurse when he was a practicing doctor in the East, comes to Tombstone to take Doc back. He will not go and becomes increasingly hostile to Wyatt as the marshal takes an interest in the girl. Just before she is to leave Tombstone at Doc's request, Wyatt takes her to the services on the foundations of the new church.

Wyatt suspects Old Man Clanton and his four sons of rustling his cattle, but when he finds his brother's medal on Doc's Mexican girlfriend, Chihuahua, he arrests Doc as James's murderer. Chihuahua then admits that one of the Clanton boys gave her the medal, and at that moment she is shot by Billy Clanton, who has been watching from outside her window. Virgil Earp chases the fatally wounded Billy to the Clanton place, where Virgil is killed by Old Man Clanton.

Back in Tombstone, Doc's operation to save Chihuahua seems successful, but as the Earp brothers wait for dawn to accept the Clantons' challenge at the OK Corral, Doc joins them because Chihuahua has died. In the ensuing shoot-out, the entire Clanton family and Doc Holliday are killed.

Clementine Carter stays in Tombstone to be the school-marm, and Wyatt and Morgan ride away to take their brothers' bodies home to their father. They say goodbye to her on the road leading out of Tombstone.

I n all Ford's films there is an element of legend. This is especially true of the Westerns, in which a whole body of mythology has been created. *My Darling Clementine* is unique among Ford's Westerns, however, in dealing with a specific and personal legend (Wyatt Earp and Doc Holliday) and expanding it to a larger Western myth. In films like *The Iron Horse* and the cavalry pictures, Ford works within the general legend of the cavalry or the building of the railroad. In other films, like *The Man Who Shot Liberty Valance,* the legend is created within the film. In *Three Godfathers* Ford creates his own parable and allegory. The story and characters in *My Darling Clementine* might seem limiting and restrictive, but Ford uses the viewer's already established awareness of the legend to enhance the myth he is creating.

The opening of the film, with the introduction of the Earp brothers, immediately establishes this mythical quality through the spare, expressionistic visual style that characterizes the film. Each brother is introduced in a low-angle medium shot, alone on his horse driving the cattle. First is James, the youngest and the first to die, and last is Wyatt. These shots prepare for the acting out of the legend that will follow.

The setting is Monument Valley, which immediately isolates the story (in time, history, and locale) and creates a closed world for it to work within.

James's grave is out in the valley, not in Tombstone's Boot Hill. When Wyatt goes out to talk to him, he goes alone to the desert and is shown against the sky and a monument. He tells James that someday this country will be a good place, "where boys like you can grow up safe." The valley is a stage for Wyatt's pledge to his dead brother and adds a sense of purpose to the boy's death.

Perhaps the strongest effect of the visual style in creating the myth is the sense of inevitability it carries with it. When Wyatt and old Mr. Clanton (and his son Ike) meet, they size each other up in a way that foreshadows the eventual shootout, and this foreboding is not found in anything they say. It is conveyed in the camera angles, compositions, and lengths of individual shots and from this expressive scene we feel the same sense of impending doom as when Macbeth meets the witches on the moor. Later, after James has been killed, there is a second fateful meeting in which Wyatt tells the Clantons he is going to stay on as marshal. They laugh at the very idea of a marshal in Tombstone, and as an afterthought they ask his name. When he answers, "Earp, Wyatt Earp," we see only the Clantons and the effect the name has on them. In this way, Ford develops the sense of inevitability, of the eventual clash between them from which only one can emerge.

The death of James is handled in this expressionistic style from the very beginning. In the dinner scene around the campfire, James's brothers fondly tease his innocence, and a reference is made to his impending marriage. For him to die is more than for a member of their family to die—he is the only one with this kind of innocence and this kind of future. With him dies the promise of an easy and uncomplicated future. Avenging his death is more than family revenge; it is the destruction of that which stands in the way of such innocence enduring in this world, and it is the purification of the enclosed world of the legend. His death is therefore necessary in a more important way than simply for plot requirements; it sets the rationale for the entire legend.

The character of Wyatt Earp by itself is of legendary proportions. It is perhaps the best use of Henry Fonda's special persona ever realized. Fonda has a withdrawn, rigid side of his character that can be filled in many ways. In *The Grapes of Wrath* Ford keeps him lacking in personality, making him a vessel into which the "I'll be there" speech, through which he comes to stand for all the oppressed workers of the Depression, can be poured. In *Fort Apache* he is kept empty, lacking in personality or ability to relate to even his own daughter. In *Drums Along the Mohawk* his awkwardness and stiffness serve as a self-contained foil to enhance the humanity of the character he is playing. This wooden quality is used in a similar way in *My Darling Clementine*, but the implications of the lonelier aspects of his persona are

Wyatt Earp and the Clantons: the inevitability of conflict.

Marshal Wyatt Earp.

On the set of *My Darling Clementine*.

also developed. He is always isolated, even from his brothers. Morgan and Virgil go to see James together, but Wyatt goes alone.

Wyatt is legendary in his abilities. He is calm and sure of himself throughout, and whatever he chooses to do, he does with relative ease, as if he were simply acting out his part in the legend. The very lack of any questioning of his capabilities enhances the legendary implications of the character. He is not simply a character; he is a force.

At the same time, however, Wyatt is one of Ford's most charming, human characters. This is what makes the film so powerful—it works well both at the personal-story level and at the level of mythology. The two are so well balanced and integrated that they never interfere with each other. The often-mentioned little dance he does against the post as he sits in his usual place outside the hotel, watching people coming and going in his town, is an inspirational touch. His inactive, watchful pose is given a charm and flavor that actors playing out a legend almost never achieve.

The Earp and Clanton families are similar in some ways. Both have only a father; in neither is there even the mention of a mother. This removes the possibility that the reason for the "evil" character of the Clanton family is the absence of a mother. It seems more that the Clantons represent an unnatural manifestation of the institution of family that must be eradicated. They look forward to the Cleggs of *Wagonmaster* in that they are ugly, they are stupid (except for Old Man Clanton), they engage in crime, and there are some hints of perversion (which are developed in *Wagonmaster*). In the scene in which Old Man Clanton and Wyatt talk out in the valley, Ike sits beside his father, mute and expressionless. He looks more bestial than human, and this idea is reinforced when the father whips his grown sons in the bar for allowing Wyatt to humiliate them. They are never seen together as a unit, as the Earp brothers are in the campfire scene, so there is no real sense of the loss of a unit when they begin to die.

Still, there is real feeling in the family, and Old

Man Clanton cries over his dead sons as Father Earp will. He risks death for himself (or actually commits suicide) in an attempt to avenge their deaths after Wyatt has said he will not kill the old man but will let him live and feel what Earp's father will feel. The Clantons are a reflection of the Earps, even if it is an unnatural one. As in classical and Shakespearean tragedy, the unnaturalness of the family, not their crime, is the real sin. The crime is simply the justification in narrative terms for the ritual killing of the unnatural family so that the natural one can survive.

Tombstone goes through a "civilization" process after Wyatt takes over as marshal. When the three brothers first ride into the little town, it is just what Old Man Clanton says it is, wide open. When Wyatt finds he cannot even get a shave in peace, he asks twice, "What kind of a town is this?" It is transformed from the "fine town" in the Clantons' terms to a civilized town of schools and churches by the presence of the Earps, through the working out of their personal problems, which have ramifications on the entire film. The wildness of Tombstone is exemplified by the drunken Indian whom no one in the town has power to control. Only Wyatt, who is untouched by the savagery and unnaturalness of the town, can rid it of this scourge. Later, under his influence, the foundations for a church go up, and the foundations are laid for the kind of town James could have grown up in.

The barber-dentist represents Eastern values struggling to make themselves felt in the West. He is a

The unnatural family of the Clantons.

Wyatt and Morgan.

Wyatt on the porch: relaxed, watchful, charming.

63

The wild town of Tombstone: Wyatt trying to get a shave.

Wyatt subdues Indian Joe.

Wyatt accepts the job of marshal of Tombstone after the death of his brother.

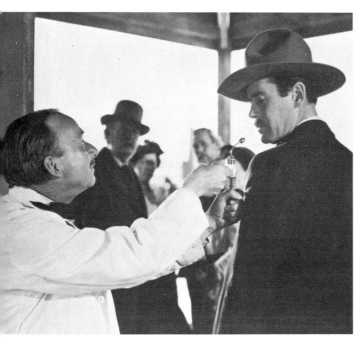

Wyatt and the blessings of civilization: the eastern barber.

little man who wants to make the most of his skills, insisting on various services (haircut, bath) that Wyatt doesn't want in the first scene. Later, however, after the appearance of Clementine Carter, Wyatt does go the whole way and is styled, washed, and perfumed by the barber.

This transformation has been discussed by Peter Wollen and others. However, the idea of Wyatt, a man of the West, being transformed into a man of the East can be overstated with regard to this film. He is not a wild man in the beginning. His gentleness has already been felt in the scenes with his family, and all he wants from the town in the first place is the "civilized" comfort of a shave. The effects of the barber do not stay with him. When he rides away at the end he is again in his old clothes and hat, riding westward.

Earp passes between the best values of East and West with no real problem, and he is the last Fordian hero to do so. The perfection of *My Darling Clementine* lies largely in this precarious balance. Earp is a man of the West with no conflict in his character—no nostalgia for lost dreams, no naive looking forward to lost futures. He is self-contained and capable of partaking from either culture or of combining them to the very best advantage. He comes from the Western tradition with inner dignity and refinement, and he can join in the church celebration or dance with the Eastern lady without undergoing a total transformation. He does not have to choose between the value systems; he internalizes both and expresses them simultaneously.

It is the town of Tombstone that undergoes the transformation. In the beginning of the film it is wild and coarse, but by the end it is the home of a church and a school. In the beginning Clementine looks frail and out of place in such a town, but by the end she is the schoolmarm, and the town has enlarged to encompass the values she represents. Earp, however, is left largely untouched by the events that have gone on. We might assume he will return to marry Clementine and become integrated into the new Tombstone, but we should be careful of doing so. His stature as a mythical, legendary figure is largely dependent on his remaining outside the course of events. At the end he remains essentially what he was at the beginning—a self-defined personality in control of events but not altered by them. As a mythical hero, he is carried along by a higher logic than is inherent in narrative-plot developments.

In the last shot he rides along a long, vertical road that extends to a distant monument, also vertical. This line charts his path—vertically into the distance of the frame, into the future. The path does not end with the monument, but rather it is carried upward into infinity by its point. Certainly Wyatt's path will not return this way. He goes away just as he came, alone, apart from the community of any society, and in some way empty, as are all larger-than-life figures who are to be filled by an implied meaning.

Doc Holliday is the third major force (besides Wyatt and the Clantons) in the film. Even before we see him there is a premonition of some kind of confrontation between him and Wyatt. When Doc first walks into the gambling saloon we feel his power through the reactions of the people, rather than by seeing Doc himself. The hands of the professional gambler pause on the money he has won as he is about to sweep it toward him. Doc's presence is felt in the oppressive silence that falls over the saloon. He walks to the end of the bar, which is cleared for him, and stands alone. People leave, and the poker game breaks up as if on signal.

Wyatt is the only man unaffected by Doc's presence. He picks up his chips, sweeping them into his hat, which he then puts on, and walks down the empty bar to Doc. As they look each other over, each is seen in a one-shot. Doc offers Wyatt a drink of champagne, then insists that he accept it. In this acceptance is some kind of acknowledgement of Doc's power, and the atmosphere relaxes. Doc then pushes his advantage and asks Wyatt if he is there to "deliver us from all evil." Wyatt replies it might not be a bad idea, and now each is shot over the other's shoulder. The tension rises, and just when Doc is going to call him out, Wyatt's brothers silently step up to the bar in the background. Morgan slides Wyatt a gun, and the power balance is tipped to Wyatt's side. Wyatt orders whiskey, and Doc accepts it. They have reached a standstill in terms of power, and with this comes a

Wyatt stops Chihuahua from packing for Clementine.

Wyatt meets Doc Holliday.

Wyatt and Clementine Carter.

friendly, mutual respect. Wyatt seems to be the only person in the film whom Doc respects, perhaps because he is the only one over whom Doc does not have power —the kind of power he wields and yet hates.

The two sides of Doc are larger than life, as in classical tragic heroes. On the one hand he was a doctor; on the other he is now a gambling boss. In his room his diploma hangs on the wall, and a whiskey bottle sits below them, like poles of good and evil balanced against each other. As Doc sits in his room drunk one night, he sees his reflection in the glass covering the diploma and throws the whiskey at it. He hates the reminder of what he has been.

Doc's torment is that he cannot come to terms with himself, and this is represented by the women in his life—Clementine Carter, Eastern, fair, respectable, and virginal; and Chihuahua, dark (Mexican or, as Wyatt refers to her, Apache), wild, unrefined, perhaps a prostitute. Doc left Clementine and came West. She followed to find out why. When they meet, she assumes that he left the East because of his health— he coughs with consumption. But the physical disease seems to be only an expression of a deeper, moral disease that torments Doc wherever he goes. He will

not return to the East with Clementine, and we finally believe him when he says that he really does not want to, that he is not simply being noble because he is physically ill.

Chihuahua is his "girl," she sings to him, loves him, and brings him whiskey and other comforts in the morning. It would seem that his affair with her is an expression of that immoral, degenerate side of him; yet when he says he will take her away with him and marry her, he seems more fully responsible and moral than he has ever been in the film. When he runs away from her, too, the women clearly are not the cause, or even the expression, of his torments. They are simply victims of them, just as he is.

Doc's basic problem is his inability to come to terms with himself and the various aspects of his life. In the soliloquy from *Hamlet,* he becomes a player in a larger drama, which takes on significance both from the play and from his life. Hearing the first lines, Doc tells Wyatt not to interrupt; he wants to hear it. As the actor goes through "to be or not to be, that is the question," Doc is drawn closer and closer, as though against his will, and the fears expressed in the speech are clearly his own. Doc has come West to escape his

Clementine and Doc: expressive darkness on his face.

The poles represented by the women: Chihuahua and Clementine.

former life and whatever "slings and arrows of outrageous fortune" plagued him there. Now that Clementine has come West, he tells her he will go farther if she will not leave. She represents his past, which he cannot live with. His suicidal drinking shows that he cannot come to terms with his present, and only through the operation does he first gain back some of his confidence in his ability to live with himself, before he loses it totally upon Chihuaha's death. When she dies, his last possibility of redemption dies with her, and he fears death less than he despises his own life. Doc takes up the speech at

Wyatt, "Mr. Shakespeare," and Doc.

> The undiscovered country, from whose bourn
> No traveller returns, puzzles the will,
> And makes us rather bear those ills we have
> Than fly to others that we know not of?
> Thus conscience does make cowards of us all,
>
> (*Hamlet* III, i, 79–83)

and he chokes with his cough and cannot continue.

Exactly what makes Doc a coward is never made clear. His torments rage in him, and only their expressions are seen on the surface in the form of his disease, the women, and the speech. With the death of Chihuahua, he makes an existential decision to face

69

Doc and Wyatt listen to Hamlet's soliloquy from outside the saloon.

what is left of his life and possibly to lose it altogether.

Doc functions as a foil to Wyatt now even more than he has previously. He is as alienated from the community as is Wyatt, and he is therefore linked with him in his solitude. As the Shakespearean actor says to his companion as he leaves the town, "Great souls by instinct to each other turn." Doc fails where Wyatt succeeds—at coming to terms with his own sense of loss and living with his solitude. He does not have the dimensions of a hero, which would enable him to do this, but through his failure we understand Wyatt's heroic proportions. When Doc dies, it is a result, not really of his wound, but of his physical infirmity (an indication of his inner moral state) which causes him to leave himself open for a moment, during which he is shot. The bullet is simply the agent of his death; the cause is his personal failure to act morally in his life. What links him with Wyatt is that the boundaries of "moral behavior" are the same for both of them, setting them apart from the rest of the characters in the film.

Doc is the character who sacrifices himself for the new civilization, not the ordinary hero (who would be Wyatt in this film) who gives up his life or his real freedom that a better world may be created. In *My Darling Clementine* each character's function grows out of his internal state. It is organic to the character and not a role he fills. In dying Doc has come to terms with his own moral state as a tragic figure, and his death is personally fulfilling as well as thematically integrated into the story. In the same way, Wyatt is carrying out (1) the requirements of plot in terms of the legend, (2) his personal destiny to avenge his

brother's death, (3) the philosophical rationale of the creation of the civilized Western community, and (4) his mythical destiny to wander solitary through life and never settle.

The dance on the foundations of the church is the culmination of all the strains of the film. It is the physical expression of the society the West can support, with all its ritualistic connotations. When the archetypal father-hero figure and his "lady fair" (the archetypal Eastern figure of purity) begin to dance, an upsweep of emotion, which has been building along the long walk down the street of Tombstone as Wyatt and Clementine approach the celebration, catches the audience and carries us along with it in a feeling created by the music and compositions of the scene. Much in this way the entire film achieves a unity of visual expression, thematic implications, and legendary fulfillment that makes it satisfying on all levels.

Underlying that satisfaction and giving it a depth and poignancy are the dark aspects of the film—the tragedy of Doc and, more importantly, Wyatt's failure to become part of the new Tombstone. Looking forward to *The Searchers,* Wyatt's inner solitude cannot be healed by the town, and in leaving he legitimizes the myth through his sacrifice.

Wyatt prevents Doc from running away from Tombstone and from himself.

70

Wyatt Earp at the OK Corral.

Wyatt Earp and Old Man Clanton.

Wyatt Earp and Clementine: the marshal and
his lady fair.

The dance on the foundations of the church.

6
FORT APACHE

CREDITS

Production company, Argosy Pictures. *Director,* John Ford. *Producers,* John Ford, Merian C. Cooper. *Script,* Frank S. Nugent; based on James Warner Bellah's story "MASSACRE." *Director of photography,* Archie Stout. *Music,* Richard Hageman. *Conductor,* Lucien Cailliet. *Editor,* Jack Murray. *Art director,* James Basevi. *Set decorator,* Joe Kish. *Costumes,* Michael Meyers (men), Ann Peck (women). *Production manager,* Bernard McEveety. *Assistant directors,* Lowell Farrell, Jack Pennick. *Second-unit director,* Cliff Lyons. *Locations filmed in Monument Valley and Mexican Hat, Utah. Released March 9, 1948. Running time,* 127 minutes. *Distributor,* RKO Radio.

CAST

John Wayne *(Captain Kirby York),* Henry Fonda *(Lieutenant Colonel Owen Thursday),* Shirley Temple *(Philadelphia Thursday),* John Agar *(Lieutenant Michael O'Rourke),* Ward Bond *(Sergeant Major O'Rourke),* George O'Brien *(Captain Sam Collingwood),* Victor McLaglen *(Sergeant Mulcahy),* Pedro Armendariz *(Sergeant Beaufort),* Anna Lee *(Mrs. Collingwood),* Irene Rich *(Mrs. O'Rourke),* Guy Kibbee *(Doctor Wilkens),* Grant Withers *(Silas Meacham),* Miguel Inclan *(Cochise),* Jack Pennick *(Sergeant Schattuck),* Mae Marsh *(Mrs. Gates), Dick Foran* (Sergeant Quincannon), Frank Ferguson *(newspaperman),* Francis Ford *(bartender),* Ray Hyke, Movita Castenada, Mary Gordon.

SYNOPSIS:

Lieutenant Colonel Thursday, an Eastern military man, takes command of Fort Apache, a Western outpost. He brings with him Philadelphia, his daughter, who is immediately drawn to young Lieutenant Michael O'Rourke, a West Point graduate just returned home to Fort Apache, where his father is the sergeant major. Thursday brings to his new post a more rigid concept of the cavalry than it has been used to, and he comes into conflict with Captain York.

The Apaches leave their reservation, and Captain York convinces Cochise to return by giving the Apache leader his word he will be listened to and treated with respect. Thursday tricks Cochise by attempting to force him to come in, and

nearly the entire cavalry command is wiped out because Thursday does not understand how to fight Indians. Before he dies, however, Thursday's bravery and commitment to his men earn him York's respect.

Years later, the heroic myth of "Thursday's charge" is carried on by York, now commander of Fort Apache. Philadelphia and Michael O'Rourke are married, and they name their baby Michael Thursday York O'Rourke.

*F*ort Apache deals with a dichotomy that runs through all John Ford's Westerns and through the genre itself—a love of individual freedom, self-sufficiency, and independence that is philosophically at odds with the need to become part of a greater whole, a mythical community whose value is greater than that of any individual. The cavalry represents the whole, but Colonel Thursday and Captain York stand at opposing extremes of that whole at the beginning of the film, and the creation of the continuing community takes place when the best characteristics of each man merge into one.

Colonel Thursday is the antithesis of individuality. He judges people by their rank or position, with no feeling for their inherent value as individuals. He is rigidly committed to the forms of the army—dress, obedience, rank—but has no understanding of the relation these forms have to the greater significance of the cavalry, and he sees them instead as ends in themselves. Colonel Thursday's cavalry is therefore a hollow one. He responds more to the substance of discipline than to its essence. He cannot get beyond the superficiality of things, and this manifests itself in a snobbery and class consciousness that is out of place in the desert of Monument Valley. He was stationed in Europe before coming to the West and reflects European values (as a critical American understands them) of appearances without understanding European depth of tradition.

Henry Fonda worked for Ford in two earlier Westerns, *Drums Along the Mohawk* and *My Darling Clementine*. In these films, Ford emphasized the human side of Fonda's persona, letting the stiff, unnatural side act as a built-in foil for his shy humanity. In *Fort Apache,* however, only the rigid elements of Fonda's abilities are used. Like the yellow cavalry stripe on his pants, he is a long, stiff, unyielding man who cannot be moved by reason or by appeal to emotion. He is linear both in his visual presence as a rigid vertical element in Ford's compositions and even in his voice, which is always flat, making his orders as lacking in humanity in their sound as in their meaning.

Philadelphia is in every way a contrast to Thursday. As his daughter, she is identified with him, is closer emotionally to him than any other person, and this closeness serves to point up his alienation more completely than it could be shown through his men. Both he and his daughter are Eastern, but she is ready to accept and try new experiences, while he is locked in the rigidity of his rank. He is awkward at showing affection to her, even of a verbal nature. Thus, when she is pleased that he is no longer stationed in Europe away from her, his unfeeling response is, "Better there than here." She succeeds in her sphere of army life (the structure of the women and their role in the community of the cavalry) better than he does in his. People immediately like her because she does not shield herself from them as Thursday does. The first morning when she tries to put the house in order she starts out full of energy but quickly becomes angry and discouraged, kicking things in the house and finally running out to find help. Her path along the joint porches of the homes is comparable to Thursday's walking through his men. Phil says, "Good morning," to everyone, turns heads, drops her hat, and is generally loose and disruptive. By contrast, Thursday never allows an inch of himself to be out of control.

Phil also offers a visual contrast to Thursday's linear quality. She represents a roundness in figure, face, and action. She is as multidirectional as he is unidirectional. She is as natural as he is unnatural in manner, speech, and feelings. She is emotional where he will not allow emotions, as when she announces her love for Michael, and Thursday coldly states that he will send her back East, where she will have two years (until she is of age) to forget him. She acts as a foil for the human side of Thursday, as York acts as a foil for the military side of the man.

Phil not only serves as a contrast for her father, but with her love of Michael she also confronts him with the superficiality of his values. The very fact that she makes a connection with another person contrasts her with her father, who remains rigid and isolated throughout the film. Visually, Michael and Phil are a couple almost upon their first meeting. They are framed together as they are introduced, with Sergeant Mulcahy smiling at them in the background. He forms the apex of the triangle formation Ford uses so meaningfully.

Michael is of the O'Rourke family, the family of the cavalry. The woman of the house is the leader of the women of the fort and their spiritual head—the most "army" of the wives. Her husband is the sergeant major, always a position of capability and character in Ford's cavalry pictures. Their son is a returning graduate of West Point, an officer. The other Irish sergeants of the post treat Mike with an easy affection, respect, and roughhousing that adds up in the end to protectiveness. They help him out when he is drilling the new recruits, because that is "no job for a gentleman," and he has become a gentleman. His

Colonel Thursday: rigidity in posture and in philosophy.

Colonel Thursday and Philadelphia arrive at Fort Apache.

Thursday and Philadelphia.

Ward Bond as Sergeant Major O'Rourke.

The Irish Sergeants: Schattuck, Mulcahy, Quincannon.

Philadelphia and Michael O'Rourke: a couple from their first meeting.

80

link between the enlisted men (his father and friends) and the officers (his new rank) offers much both in the way of comedy and in the significance of joining together the "family" of the fort.

Michael's homecoming after four years at the Point is one of the most touching scenes in the film. It is that wonderful combination of the formal and informal that only Ford can create. Michael walks in to see his father reading, and his demeanor makes clear the father's position as head of the house and authority figure for the boy. The sergeant major looks up, then quickly down for a moment to avoid showing his emotion too openly. His restraint carries with it more love than a more open show of emotion could, and he solemnly calls to his wife, "Woman of the house, your son is home."

When Mrs. O'Rourke joins them the tension is broken and they embrace, measure against each other, and the sergeant major hits Michael in the belly when he stands at attention. Mrs. O'Rourke's influence is to soften the formal aspects of the situation and bring the emotion out into the open.

It is in contrast to the O'Rourkes that Thursday's lack is most obvious. He has insulted Sergeant Major O'Rourke by observing that only sons of holders of the Medal of Honor can receive a presidential appointment to West Point. O'Rourke answers, "That was my impression too, sir," which informs the colonel that O'Rourke does indeed hold that honor. O'Rourke emerges from that encounter with even greater dignity, as both his modesty and his high accomplishments have been questioned and then affirmed.

Later, when Thursday comes to the O'Rourke house to take Phil home after she has disobeyed him by seeing Michael, Thursday again refuses to give the O'Rourkes the respect due them, and again he loses his own dignity. He is reminded that an officer cannot barge uninvited into the home of one of his men. He opposes his daughter's marriage to Michael on grounds of class: Michael's father is of lower rank than Phil's. This judgmental attitude based on superficial virtues again demeans Thursday.

One element that is lacking in Thursday and that adds immeasurably to O'Rourke is the rounding of the male character by a wife. Women are vital in unifying the Fordian community (in its function as an extended family), and they have their own place in the structure of army society. Mrs. O'Rourke is the leader of that society in the same way that her husband is in control of running the fort. She is undisputed master in the "office" that is her home, and she makes this known when her husband tries to send Phil home in accordance with her father's order. It is Mrs. O'Rourke's province, and she is without equal in it. She tells her husband in no uncertain terms that Phil will stay, and he says no more. From the tone of their speaking to each other, she and the sergeant major apparently have a formalized relationship, but their

Lieutenant Michael O'Rourke is welcomed home from West Point.

Lieutenant Michael O'Rourke and Sergeant Major O'Rourke.

The substance of honor: Thursday and O'Rourke.

support of one another and their respect for each other's spheres are evident. When Michael is sent off with the repair wagon in a gesture that seems like petty revenge and punishment, she comes up to her husband and they clasp hands for a moment.

The influence of the women in Ford's films is often shown through dances, which express the unity of the community through music and movement. Dances are the warm, human side of cavalry life, the community life of the army, and the traditional expression of a society's togetherness. Twice, Thursday interrupts dances, reinforcing his role as disrupter of the community's sense of unity. The first time is with his arrival at Fort Apache when the officers are celebrating Washington's birthday. His physical presence is an intrusion on the atmosphere of the dance but not, as might be expected, by his being dirty and dusty from the long ride. Rather, his linear quality, which is incapable of easy, relaxed fun, portrays his resentment of the gaiety and freedom of movement. He refuses to relax into the good company of the officers and his old friends the Collingwoods. When York takes Phil onto the dance floor, Thursday walks out the door and stands with his back to the company.

The second time he interrupts a dance it is the noncommissioned officers' ball, the most relaxed, enjoyable affair on the post. His calling the dance to a halt seems almost calculated in terms of its consistancy with his general effect on Fort Apache. He seems pleased to end the success of the social function, as if he resented their ability to create it. He is pleased to put the unit back to their real task — killing Indians—instead of frivolity into which he is incapable of entering.

In this dance, which almost immediately precedes the battle, the tensions come to a head between Thursday and the characters who contrast with him. Meacham, the corrupt Indian agent who continues in his post only because Thursday has more respect for the position than contempt for the man, is present, as if to echo the lack of integrity Thursday has created in the community. Primarily, however, the dance is an extended family function, and the tensions are family ones.

It is the custom that the post commander dance with the sergeant major's wife, so that the square is led off by Thursday and Mrs. O'Rourke. This most unnatural combination is joined by the sergeant major and the colonel's lady, Phil. These couples are here visually linked as representative of the O'Rourke and Thursday families, who will complete the cavalry family when they are physically one at the end of the film.

Phil, the O'Rourkes, and the women of Fort Apache are all contrasts to Thursday, but the greatest contrast is Captain Kirby York, who is not only the most individualistic of the men, but also the military contrast to Thursday's rigidity. Kirby is human where

Philadelphia comes to the O'Rourke home against her father's wishes, and he invades the family to take her home.

Thursday is not; he is capable of bending to the requirements of a situation. This is a difference of East and West as much of personality. In this country of desert and savage force, a man must deal with these elements in new ways to match new threats. York is also human; he and Phil are accepted into the O'Rourke household at dinner, indicating that both have a place Thursday does not in the family of the fort.

John Wayne's Captain York is much the same character that Wayne plays in *Rio Grande,* also named Kirby Yorke. York in *Fort Apache* is younger, less burdened by the demands of rank and responsibility. From the first moment we see him, York is the embodiment of grace and stature, combined in a way

that Thursday could never combine them. He is easy and joking with Phil (referring to her "nightle" when she greets Michael on the stairs in the morning) but strong and assertive with Thursday. At their first military meeting he disagrees with Thursday over the prowess of the Apaches, and he walks away parroting the colonel's orders to have breakfast. The two men are two different approaches to militarism and leadership—Thursday too rigid and uncompromising, York too individualistic and lacking in an understanding of the value of discipline.

Honor is one point upon which York and Thursday illustrate their different orientations. To Thursday, honor is a superficial characteristic whose limit and obligation are dictated by rank and position. When

York gives his word to Cochise, Thursday does not feel that it need be honored. Even when it is demonstrated to him that the Indian leader is decent, honorable, and admirable, he feels there is no need to honor the word because Cochise is a savage, an Indian who, regardless of provocation, has broken the treaty by leaving the reservation. The factual superficialities of the situation are all that matter to Thursday. The Indians have broken the law and must learn that they cannot disobey the United States government. Even though Cochise has done what York says "any decent man would do," that man is still an Indian and the rank and power relationship between his nation and Thursday's must be maintained.

There is a suggestion of a question of honor between Thursday and Collingwood that is never fully revealed. They knew each other once, before Collingwood came to Fort Apache, and it is hinted that Thursday had something to do with his old friend's being transferred West. When he arrives at the fort, Thursday spurns the friendship offered by Mrs. Collingwood. One role of the women in the army community is to encourage the informal by a show of emotion or a comment a man might not be able to make. Mrs. Collingwood calls Owen Thursday by his first name, an inviting gesture that her husband would be compromised in making, especially since it is refused.

Collingwood later says something about explanations—that he tried to offer one once but it was not

The Non-Commissioned Officers' Ball.

The women of Fort Apache: Philadelphia Thursday, Mrs. O'Rourke, and Mrs. Collingwood.

accepted. This hint, coupled with the later exchange in the last-stand battle with the Indians, when Collingwood says, "This time *you're* late, Owen," indicates that Thursday dealt very harshly with Collingwood when he was "late" once before (possibly with a good reason that Collingwood was not allowed to present). Collingwood has become a drunkard, but he has more humanity throughout most of the picture than Thursday has with his narrow strength. Collingwood wants desperately to leave Fort Apache, as much as does Thursday, but his wife's gesture in the end gives him a dignity that is equivalent to the sacrifice of his life.

The battle itself is a study in what Peter Bogdanovich has called Ford's glory in defeat. What lives after that massacre is not Colonel Thursday or his men, but

Captain York and the Apaches.

York and Cochise.

Thursday and Collingwood.

Thursday and Cochise.

York, Meacham, and Thursday.

a tradition more important than any of them. That they will be defeated is fairly evident as they ride way from the fort. As they sing "She Wore a Yellow Ribbon" and other traditional cavalry songs, they sweep by the camera in a mythical unity. They cut into the landscape of the valley in a line, comprising a force that cannot again separate into individuals.

The meeting with Cochise is destined to failure—they meet in a formally composed shot with a monument behind them, as immovable as Thursday. The formal perfection of the composition in these scenes creates the feeling of inevitability, of two forces moving toward a collision that cannot be halted or prevented. The situation is so powerful that its tragedy is transcended by the force of destiny. There is more power in living out a myth than in winning a battle, and this is the key to many Ford films. The men die to create the myth; York and Michael must live to report it and keep it alive, and the last scene explains it and confirms its rightful power and importance.

In this last scene Kirby has internalized many of Thursday's best qualities, which make him less loose and free but better fit for the demands of leadership. This is most obvious in his putting on the desert cap Thursday wore in the last stand, but it is also evident in his manner, his stance, and the camera angles used to place him. He stands in the frame almost as stiff and rigid as Thursday did, and he speaks in as certain terms of the requirements of his job, regardless of how he may feel about them.

By allowing the lie of Thursday's heroic military leadership and death to go unchallenged, Kirby is bowing to the needs of rank and superficial criteria of honor and ability. But it is vitally important that the troop have a hero in its immediate past, and Kirby is now able to see the greater good, to which he would have not given in earlier. It is a lesson he learned from Thursday on the battlefield, along with, "When you lead this troop, mister, and I expect you will shortly, *lead* it." That is one thing Thursday always does. It often makes him look and act incorrectly, since he ignores valuable advice or better-informed opinions, but he does lead it, and the men never have any doubt who their commanding officer is. That is why they will stand with him and die with him.

One has the feeling that if Thursday had a wife he would be more flexible. This is Ford's general view; women are humanizing influences in the West. They remind men what they are fighting for and make them keep hold of some of their human qualities while they tame the land. Phil is not enough for Thursday, but she will be for Michael. Michael Thursday York O'Rourke, Phil's and Michael's baby, is a conglomeration of them all and symbolizes the ultimate purpose of Fort Apache—the growth of families which make up a community that will survive and make the West a good place in which to live.

In the last analysis it is the cavalry that stirs Ford's deepest feelings in *Fort Apache.* The shot of York through the window, with the reflection of the dead troopers in the glass over him while he speaks of the cavalry that will go on and on, is one of Ford's most moving. He says that the names change, but the cavalry remains the same; it is a unity that is more than the sum of its parts, more important than any

The battle:

The Apaches.

The "fact": Thursday defeated.

The "legend": The glory of Thursday's Charge.

one of them. Thursday's contribution was to "make them better men," as York tells the reporters, and to add to them a measure of respect for the glue of discipline that holds the cavalry together. He brought to Fort Apache a formalizing, rigid interpretation of the rules, regulations, and traditions that, when fused with the person of Captain York, did make the regiment a better one.

In *Fort Apache* the character of Kirby York is capable of merging (but not submerging) his individuality with the greater whole of the cavalry and assimilating the qualities of Thursday necessary for a leader. The army, especially the cavalry, has always (until recently) had a sentimental emotional value for Americans because of the idea of sacrifice. First a soldier sacrifices his individuality to the greater whole by putting on a uniform and taking a rank that groups him with others. Then he may be moved to a greater sacrifice—his life. Sacrifice for something greater than one's own life and happiness has always been an ideal, but such sacrifice does not have the same emotional impact when it is done alone. To an American mind, the sacrifice of individuality is the first and perhaps the greatest that can be made.

Often the tension between contradictions that exist in the same person, especially in the same artistic sensibility, makes for the great emotional depth of ambiguity in an artistic work. This is one of those tensions in John Ford—a great love and respect for individuality, independent acion, and self-sufficiency, yet a great need to submerge one's hard-won individuality to a larger mythical whole. From this springs his great feeling for community, especially the community of the cavalry.

In Ford's later works he realizes the impossibility of successfully combining these two ideals, and more and more his characters embody either one quality or the other. Characters' attempts to combine the two impulses are seen in *Fort Apache,* and more successfully in *Rio Grande* and *Wagonmaster,* but they have failed by *Two Rode Together.* In *The Man Who Shot Liberty Valance,* there is an artistic awareness at work that counters the bitterness of realization evident in *Two Rode Together* and reaches new heights of feeling for the side of Ford that finally shows as most meaningful—the individual.

In *Drums Along the Mohawk,* the farmer can become a fighter and go back to being a farmer with no questioning of where his values lie or how he can best express them. As Ford's Westerns progress, a more definite structure is required to give his heroes that meaning, and the cavalry becomes the prominent structure of the 1949–60 Westerns. After that this structure is abandoned, because even its mythology is not great enough to give that certainty of wholeness and purpose with which Ford needs to imbue his lead characters.

Fort Apache is the first of the Westerns to deal with this cavalry theme, and in it is the simplest and most uncomplicated expression of the theme. The ideal of the cavalry is never brought into question, only individuals within it. Methodology is questioned, not the mythology behind it. The purity of the last shot is not to be repeated in the cavalry pictures: the firm belief expressed visually that there is a oneness about the cavalry, a wholeness that makes the sacrifice of individuality worthwhile. The men are not even remembered by their names except for Thursday, who is remembered as something he was not. Never again is Ford so sure about the sacrifice of the individual.

7
THREE GODFATHERS

CREDITS

Production company, Argosy Pictures. *Director,* John Ford. *Producers,* John Ford, Merian C. Cooper. *Script,* Laurence Stallings, Frank S. Nugent. *Story,* Peter P. Boyle. *Director of photography,* Winton C. Hoch. Color process, Three-Color Technicolor. *Second-unit photography,* Charles P. Boyle. *Color consultants,* Natalie Kalmus, Morgan Padelford. *Special effects,* Jack Caffee. *Music,* Richard Hageman. *Conductor,* Lucien Cailliet. *Editor,* Jack Murray. *Art director,* James Basevi. *Set decorator,* Joe Kish. *Production manager,* Lowell Farrell. *Assistant directors,* Wingate Smith, Edward O'Fearna. *Locations filmed in the Mojave Desert. Released December 1, 1948. Running time,* 106 minutes. *Remake of Ford's own* MARKED MEN *(Universal, 1919) and* THREE GODFATHERS *(MGM, 1936). Dedicated "To the memory of Harry Carey—bright star of the early western sky." Distributor,* MGM.

CAST

John Wayne *(Robert Marmaduke Sangster Hightower),* Pedro Armendariz *(Pedro Roca Fuerte),* Harry Carey, Jr. *(William Kearney, "the Abilene Kid"),* Ward Bond *(Perley "Buck" Sweet),* Mildred Natwick *(mother),* Charles Halton *(Mr. Latham),* Jane Darwell *(Miss Florie),* Mae Marsh *(Mrs. Sweet),* Guy Kibbee *(judge),* Dorothy Ford *(Ruby Latham),* Ben Johnson, Michael Dugan, Don Summers *(deputies),* Fred Libby *(deputy sheriff),* Hank Worden *(deputy sheriff),* Jack Pennick *(Luke, train conductor),* Francis Ford *(drunk).*

SYNOPSIS:

Robert Hightower, Pedro Fuerte, and William Kearney, "the Abilene Kid," ride into Welcome, Arizona, to rob the bank. Without knowing he is the sheriff, they talk with Buck Sweet, and he pursues them into the desert after the robbery. The three outlaws head for Tarapin Tanks, where they find a tenderfoot has blown up the water tanks and left his pregnant wife alone in their wagon. They become the newborn boy's godfathers, promising the dying woman to save her baby.

A Bible instructs them to take the child to New Jerusalem, and they set out by night, following a star. "The Kid" and Pedro both die on the way, leaving Bob alone to save the child.

When he, too, collapses, they return in song and shadow to urge him on. Just when he can go no farther, he finds a donkey prophesied by the Bible to take the child to New Jerusalem on Christmas Eve.

He is met there by Buck Sweet, who takes him back to Welcome to stand trail for robbing the bank. He gets one year in prison, while Mr. and Mrs. Sweet care for his godson until he is free.

In *Three Godfathers* the ritual of sacrifice and redemption is acted out in the American West using Christian symbols and parables. The theme of sacrifice, generally of an individual for a greater good, is very clear in most of Ford's Westerns. For anything of real value to be achieved, something of great value must be given up. This concept has roots in agrarian death-and-rebirth ritual and in pagan religion, but Ford's choice to set its symbolism within the very explicit framework of Christian mythology indicates his preoccupation with that subject.

There are basically two parables in *Three Godfathers*. More explicit of the two is the Christmas story with the birth of the baby on Christmas day, the following of the star, and the safe arrival in (New) Jerusalem. By becoming his godfathers and dedicating their lives to him, all three men are redeemed through the child. In the beginning of the film, when they go into the desert to escape from the town they have just robbed, their journey to redemption roughly parallels Christ's. They immediately face a sandstorm, which begins the process of stripping them down, leaving them defenseless to discover the child. The wagon Bob finds at Tarapin Tanks is mysterious and set apart from its surroundings. The wind is blowing around it as nowhere else, and it looks alone and defenseless.

Bob discovers the mother but goes back and sends Pedro to care for her. Pedro has more faith and is thereby better able to approach the "madonna." As he approaches the wagon, he looks as though he were going into a church. He goes quietly, hat in hand, and as he looks into the wagon, he is framed by the hill behind him and the curved outline of the wagon arch in a Renaissance religious composition.

After the baby has been born the three men approach the wagon in great respect and awe. They take off their hats and gunbelts and enter the wagon as though it were a cathedral. The compositions of the shots continue to develop the religious imagery, with the arch window of the back entrance always prominent in the frame with the little hill behind it. The mother asks them all to be godfathers, and they agree separately, each taking an oath of commitment. They form a circle around the child in his mother's lap, much like the Renaissance paintings whose color and composition always encircle the baby Jesus.

Pedro acts much like an initiate in this ritual, perhaps because of his own religious convictions. He is a tool, whereas Bob is the one upon whom the real miracle is worked. The Kid is in a similar position to Pedro; he is quick to accept the God-determined nature of their situation, pointing out the Bible passage that will lead them and understanding his own role as one of the three wise men. It is Bob who has no belief before this time, even joking that the tanks will be dry even if it "rains from now till I get religion."

The naming of the child is part of the ritual of acceptance. He is christened Robert William Pedro Hightower, beginning and ending with Bob. Their positions in the name of the child indicate their relative importance in a religion that seeks the one "lost sheep" and values its return to the fold above the ninety-nine that were never lost. Thus, Bob is first in the child's name, then the Kid, and last Pedro. This name becomes a point of comedy among them, with each calling the child by enough of its name to include his own.

When the mother dies, her baby's name is the last word on her lips, and the shot looks out the arch window, with a lantern very prominent in the frame. A wind comes up and blows the lantern out as though it were her spirit, leaving the shot in silhouette, with the shape of the lantern and the hill behind it inside the arch of the wagon. They bury the mother on the little hill that has formed the second arch in the wagon-window composition. This is the first step in their religious initiation. The Kid sings "Shall We Gather at the River" for her (the song will later return to Bob when he most needs spiritual help), and Bob says the "Amen." This action, with each man standing still and unmoving, Pedro praying, the Kid singing, and Bob watching over it all, is taken in long shot, a composition that intensifies the ritual. Ford uses this formation and camera angle when staging rituals (*The Searchers* has an almost identical scene) to formalize them. Bob, the tallest, stands between the others on the little hill, with the camera looking up at them, freezing the burial in a formalized tableau.

Later that night, Bob has a moment of doubt concerning his mission with the baby. This causes an argument in which Pedro draws his gun and the baby wakes. The drawn gun is the most prominent article in the foreground of the frame, heightening the sense of danger to the child and to the three men. The Bible, tossed aside by Bob, has fallen open to a passage telling them that the Christ child was taken to Jerusalem, and in the desert, there are Damascus, Cairo, and New Jerusalem around them.

As the Kid reads the Bible, the others leave the frame and he is left in the middle, lighted from behind, shining and in low angle. His innocent faith convinces Bob that they should try it, and the three set out for New Jerusalem. As they walk, the Kid sees

95

The three godfathers: Christmas story in the desert.

Bob Hightower, "The Abilene Kid," and Pedro after their escape from Welcome, Arizona.

The outlaws approach Tarapin Tanks.

Pedro before the wagon: as though he were going to church.

Bob tells Pedro and the Kid what he has found in the wagon.

Caring for the godchild.

Bob squeezes water from a barrel cactus.

The burial of the mother.

the star in the west that will lead them, and they walk in single file across the sand, shown in long shot, cutting to a last shot of the grave and the wagon.

Pedro and the Kid die in the desert as a sacrifice for the child's life and Bob's redemption. As the three walk across the salt flats, we are made to feel their torture as Ford cuts between shots tracking along with their feet, long shots of them approaching and seeming to advance very slowly, and a masterful setup in which the camera is almost on the ground as Bob (the first in the single-file line) approaches. We see his feet, then tilt up to see the rest of him as he passes, then, without a cut, tilt back down to catch the feet of the next man in the line and than the last. There are cuts back to Buck and his men with shorter intervals between them, to heighten the threat that comes both from the land and from their pursuers.

Finally the Kid falls and gives Pedro the Bible to read for him. As he reads, the Kid tries to say the Lord's Prayer, but instead recites "Now I Lay Me Down to Sleep." As he prays he becomes psychologically younger and younger, until at the end he is asking the Lord to make him a good boy. In this state of innocence and purification through ordeal, he dies.

Bob and the child: ready to give up.

A miracle foretold by the Bible: the donkey and her colt.

Having brought the child to New Jerusalem, Bob collapses from his ordeal.

Before the robbery, Bob tries to make the Kid pull out.

The outlaws joke with Buck Sweet before they know he is town marshal.

Mrs. Sweet mothers The Abilene Kid.

Comedy: the banker's daughter comes home.

Chasing the outlaws out of town.

THE PURSUIT

Swearing in deputies for the chase across the desert.

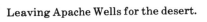

Leaving Apache Wells for the desert.

Buck Sweet finds his niece dead in her wagon.

Bob holds his hat to shade the dying boy from the murderous sun, and when the Kid dies it is signaled by the return of the sun to his face as Bob removes his hat.

Pedro dies next, and Bob remembers that the next day is Christmas. It requires the return of both the Kid and Pedro in hallucinations to keep Bob going, along with a final gesture of faith of his own, when he goes to the Bible for his next move. He does not believe what he reads, but then in an unearthly light, he sees the donkey and its colt. To swelling religious music, he leans on the donkey and soon comes to the town. In the saloon, the people of New Jerusalem are singing Christmas carols, and they all stop to marvel over the baby. Buck comes in just moments behind him, and Bob turns to greet him and falls to the floor, his trial finally over.

The second parable in *Three Godfathers*, closely woven with the first, is the parable of the prodigal son. This idea seems particularly significant to Ford, who generally gives his heroes a questionable background (*My Darling Clementine, Wagonmaster, The Searchers, Two Rode Together*) or a questionable present (*Straight Shooting, Three Bad Men, Three Godfathers*). It is as though redemption means infinitely more to someone who has had a choice, who has known the attractions, the power, and the dissatisfaction of a life of crime, cynicism, or immorality. This very knowledge deepens the character and makes his redemption more valuable than it would be to the innocent who has never known doubt. It is the doubt that makes the prodigal son value that innocence so highly and dedicate his life to its maintenance (Wyatt in *My Darling Clementine* at the grave of his young brother James). In Ford's films, the goals of a society that can support churches, schools, education, and families are those he affirms and strives to create; yet his deepest affinity always lies with characters who have known more than innocence and decency. Those characters give the society its real value—both by being strong enough to fight for it and by knowing what its value is. The wisdom of experience, the nostalgic loss of innocence, arriving at an appreciation of real values through living without them, and giving up those values for the greater good of society —these are the experiences to which Ford gives the greatest emotional depth.

Bob, then, is the outlaw for whom the mother, the Kid, and Pedro all die. His redemption is valued above their lives, or rather, their lives are given value through their effect upon his own. *Three Godfathers* is thus unusual in Ford's *oeuvre* in that it is not the individual who sacrifices for the rest of society, but they who sacrifice for his redemption. Perhaps it is this important difference that makes *Three Godfathers* a less substantial film than many of Ford's other Westerns—Bob does not have the depth of an Ethan

The trial: one year penance.

Seeing Bob off to jail: the Sweets care for his godson.

Bob leaving for jail: taking care of the deputy.

The kindly law: Buck Sweet and his prisoner Bob playing chess.

Edwards or a Tom Doniphon, both of whom see clearly and choose their existential lack of grace.

Three Godfathers has even more comedy than most of Ford's Westerns. Without the comedy, either the heavy religious symbolism or the threat of the pursuing posse would weigh too ponderously on the film. As it is, because of the good-natured comedy around Buck Sweet, the power of the law does not overwhelm the story. The careful blending of comic and serious elements is evident in the men's first meeting with Buck. He seems impotent as he works in his garden and takes their ribbing, until the scene suddenly changes, first in the music and then in the visual composition when he puts on his vest, on which is his sheriff's badge.

Comfortable medium shots of the characters talking and joking together have predominated. Now suddenly there are closeups of each outlaw in succession as he realizes Buck is the marshal. The veneer of hospitality and gentleness that is so often a mark of weakness remains intact while the illusion of weakness vanishes, taking nothing of the earlier charm of the scene with it.

Tension, either from the necessities of plot (the chase) or from the parable and the possibility of the failure of Bob's redemption, is never allowed to become very strong. Ford accomplishes this balance by making the representative of the law benign and kindly instead of stern and vindictive and by drawing so totally on Christian mythology and imagery that there can be no question of the outcome. In this way, the meaning of the parable is constantly the single most powerful idea in both the visual and the narrative content of the film. Thus, the concept of sacrifice, the key to so many of Ford's films, is expressed perhaps more explicitly in *Three Godfathers* than in any other film. The woman, the Kid, and Pedro all die so that a child may live and so that one man might be redeemed.

Christmas in New Jerusalem.

106

8
SHE WORE A YELLOW

CREDITS

Production company, Argosy Pictures. *Director,* John Ford. *Producers,* John Ford, Merian C. Cooper. *Associate producer,* Lowell Farrell. *Script,* Frank S. Nugent, Laurence Stallings; based on James Warner Bellah's story "WAR PARTY." *Director of photography,* Winton C. Hoch. *Color process,* Three-Color Technicolor. *Second-unit photography,* Charles P. Boyle. *Color consultants,* Natalie Kalmus, Morgan Padelford. *Special effects,* Jack Cosgrove, Jack Caffee. *Music,* Richard Hageman. *Conductor,* Constantine Bakaleinihoff. *Orchestrations,* Lucien Cailliet. *Editor,* Jack Murray. *Assistant editor,* Barbara Ford. *Art director,* James Basevi. *Set decorator,* Joe Kish. *Costumes,* Michael Meyers (men), Ann Peck (women). *Assistant directors,* Wingate Smith, Edward O'Fearna. *Second-unit director,* Cliff Lyons. *Locations filmed in Monument Valley, Utah. Released October 22, 1949. Running time,* 103 minutes. *One shot was used in Ford's* CHEYENNE AUTUMN *(Warner Bros., 1964). Distributor,* RKO Radio.

CAST

John Wayne *(Captain Nathan Brittles),* Joanne Dru *(Olivia Dandridge),* John Agar *(Lieutenant Flint Cohill),* Ben Johnson *(Sergeant Tyree),* Harry Carey, Jr. *(Lieutenant Pennell),* Victor McLaglen *(Sergeant Quincannon),* Mildred Natwick *(Mrs. Allshard),* George O'Brien *(Major Allshard),* Arthur Shields *(Doctor O'Laughlin),* Francis Ford *(barman),* Harry Woods *(Karl Rynders),* Chief Big Tree *(Pony That Walks),* Noble Johnson *(Red Shirt),* Cliff Lyons *(Trooper Cliff),* Tom Tyler *(Quayne),* Michael Dugan *(Hochbauer),* Mickey Simpson *(Wagner),* Fred Graham *(Hench),* Frank McGarth *(trumpeter),* Don Summers *(Jenkins),* Fred Libby *(Colonel Krumrein),* Jack Pennick *(sergeant major),* Billy Jones *(courier),* Bill Gettinger *(officer),* Fred Kennedy *(Badger),* Rudy Bowman *(Private Smith),* Post Park *(officer),* Ray Hyke *(McCarthy),* Lee Bradley *(interpreter),* Chief Sky Eagle, Dan White.

SYNOPSIS:

Just after the Little Big Horn, Captain Nathan Brittles sets out on his last mission before his retirement. His patrol, whose purpose is to find and contain the Indians who have murdered the paymaster and are amassing for a large attack, is encumbered by Miss Dandridge and her aunt. The Eastern girl is not "army" enough to stay at the Western fort for the

RIBBON

winter, and the risk to the women prevents Brittles from stopping the Indians from gathering, obtaining repeating rifles, and killing settlers. He cannot even get the women to the stagecoach.

They return to the fort, having left young Lieutenant Cohill guarding a river crossing. Brittles cannot go back for him because he will be a civilian by the next midnight, so young Lieutenant Pennell will set out the next day to effect the rescue. Captain Brittles's troop gives him a silver watch in a ceremony before they leave without him.

Brittles leaves the fort, rejoins his command, and gives orders for them to wait while he rides into the Indian camp. There he talks to old Pony That Walks, who cannot control his young braves under Red Shirt and who advises Brittles that he can do nothing to stop the coming war. Brittles waits until night; then he and his unit stampede the Indians' pony herd and thus prevent the war. His retirement now a fact, Brittles rides westward but is stopped by Sergeant Tyree, who brings him his appointment as head of civilian scouts, with the rank of colonel. They return to the fort, where Brittles goes to the graves of his family.

John Wayne as Captain Nathan Brittles.

She Wore a Yellow Ribbon is a symphony for the ears and a canvas for the eyes more than a narrative for the mind. The feelings of longing and loss, of a better past than present, and of the dignity of the men who are passing are conveyed through the sounds and scenes of the film, not through the themes of the story.

We never see the past that is implicitly mourned in *She Wore a Yellow Ribbon*: the present offers only tantalizing hints of what it must have been, making the sense of loss a gentle, diffused, all-pervasive atmosphere. Captain Brittles goes out to the graves in Monument Valley to be with his wife, Mary, and his two daughters, and Miss Dandridge is seen as a pale reflection of what his wife was to him. They both "wore a yellow ribbon"—Miss Dandridge in her hair for one of the young lieutenants, or perhaps for Captain Brittles himself; Mary's ribbon frames her photograph. When Miss Dandridge comes to see Brittles in the graveyard, the entire scene is bathed in a red, unnatural light. The set itself is on a sound stage, with a painted backdrop of a monument rising up behind the little cemetery. The impression is one of unreality, and when her shadow rises up on Mary's tombstone, we are as close to the unreal past as is possible.

The illusion of that unreal past gives it more emotional impact than the actual depiction of an idealized past possibly could. As in *Wagonmaster*, Ford only hints at an idealized reality; he shows only its effect on people, not its actuality. Its reflection, on the people who remember it in *She Wore a Yellow Ribbon*, and on the people who anticipate it in *Wagonmaster*, carries more emotion than does, for example, the idealized present of *Drums Along the*

Captain Brittles at his wife and daughters' graves in Monument Valley.

110

Miss Olivia Dandridge and Captain Brittles.

Sergeant Quincannon, Sergeant Tyree, and Major Allshard

The bugler.

Mohawk. The difference between *She Wore a Yellow Ribbon* and *Wagonmaster* is that in the earlier film the perspective is looking back, while in *Wagonmaster* it is looking forward. This is why *She Wore a Yellow Ribbon* is one of Ford's earliest really dark films.

In spite of being filmed mostly on location, *She Wore a Yellow Ribbon* has an artificial quality in addition to having a dark, brooding mood. The deep red light, which pervades night scenes and is behind the morning bugler as he announces another day closer to Brittles's retirement, anticipates *Sergeant Rutledge* with its connotations of greater darkness. The storm over the valley as they march to Sudrose Wells darkens even the exterior location and, like the artificiality of the red-lighted shots, imparts great unnatural beauty.

The burial of Trooper Smith combines the aspects of mourning over a better past, which passes with great dignity, and of the darkness we are then left with. Part of this past is the South, represented both by the old man and by Sergeant Tyree. As he dies, the old trooper is accorded great respect by Captain Brittles and by Tyree, whom he calls "Captain Tyree," his rank in the Confederate army. It is night when he is buried, and the three Southern members of the cavalry, led by Sergeant Tyree, give the late brigadier general the honors accorded a fallen Southern commander. The scene is composed with a hill behind the ceremony, instead of taking place on the hill, as is usually the case in Ford's rituals. The men are close to the camera, with the hill and sentry behind, giving the ritual immediate, personal impact rather than formal, social significance. In this film there is no community capable of receiving that significance and making it fulfill the people's greater needs, so the ritual becomes filled with deep regret and loss, instead of anticipating the future.

It is common in modern art for traditional rituals to be depicted as empty and meaningless, but even in Ford's darkest films these rituals retain a deeply personal value. They are meaningful in existential terms; their enactment affirms and justifies them without necessarily relating to the "greater value" of the community as a whole. The tension between the belief in the significance of lives such as Trooper Smith's and the absence of any tangible evidence to substantiate that belief keeps the emotional impact of *She Wore a Yellow Ribbon* elusive but always charged.

Nathan Brittles is the leader of the community of the cavalry, Ford's oft-used metaphor for the social community. Yet in *She Wore a Yellow Ribbon,* as in *The Horse Soldiers,* that community is not one that joins men and gives their lives and endeavors significance. Brittles is the most alienated individual in the film. He has lost his wife and daughters (an indication of the inadequacy of the community if it could not provide protection for the family of its

The death of the southern general, "Trooper Smith."

Captain Brittles and Sergeant Quincannon: the threat of retirement.

leader), and he is not really close to anyone except Sergeant Quincannon, with whom he shares the impending doom of being cut off from his only "family" by retirement. His relationship with Major Allshard is an echo of Lieutenant Colonel Yorke's relationship with General Sheridan in *Rio Grande,* but it lacks the core of their working together for a meaningful goal. In the later film, fulfilling the goals of the community heals Yorke's personal family wounds as well (reuniting him with Kathleen), while in *She Wore a Yellow Ribbon* such a possibility does not even exist. Thus, his relationship with his commanding officer is devoid of any real goal, making the gentle humor and conflict over the mission between them superficial.

The only real exchange of feeling Brittles has with his men is in the ceremony in which they give him a silver watch on his retirement, and it is significant that the sentiment inscribed on the watch is "Lest we forget"—again, it is the past that is of value, with the future holding nothing. It would seem that Brittles might have a future when he is not retired after all, but promoted to colonel and kept on at the fort as head of civilian scouts. But when he does return, he leaves the dance of the company and goes out to the artificial graveyard where his family lies, thus giving up the living present and future for the dead but more meaningful past.

Captain Brittles and Major Allshard.

Brittles, Allshard, and "old iron pants."

Brittles on the morning of his retirement.

The gift from his men: "lest we forget."

The passing of command, a theme of *Fort Apache,* is dealt with in a much less optimistic way in *She Wore a Yellow Ribbon.* It appears that Lieutenant Cohill will take over Captain Brittles's command, but when Tyree, Pennell, and Brittles watch the Indians killing the corrupt Indian agent and his man, a link is made between Brittles and Pennell that is developed later in the film. Brittles offers Pennell a "chaw," which is refused by Tyree but accepted by Pennell when Brittles tells him "it's been known to turn a man's stomach," giving the young lieutenant an excuse for being sick at the barbarous display before him.

It is at this point that Pennell decides not to resign from the cavalry after all. He renounces the advantages of an easy life of wealth in the East for the nebulous (especially in this film) values of the army, and it is peculiar to *She Wore a Yellow Ribbon* that his losing Miss Dandridge to Lieutenant Cohill also brings him closer to Brittles and makes him fit to take over the older man's role. Miss Dandridge has represented Mary Brittles and the past that holds all value for Nathan; yet for Pennell, losing the girl has more meaning than winning her, and he becomes a solitary individual.

In the final dance sequence, Lieutenant Cohill fades into the background with Olivia on his arm while Lieutenant Pennell turns his back to the company as Brittles has just done and stands staring out into the darkness alone. There is greater meaning (in terms of what could have been, therefore what has not been exposed to the scrutiny of reality) in the loss of the girl and his resulting alienation from the community that dances behind him than there is in Cohill's forming a family with her. In this film, Ford's hero who loses everything, and thereby gains an internal rationale greater than any the community could provide, appears in his first well-delineated form.

Sergeant Tyree is like Brittles in that he is cut off from every form of meaningful social contact except what ritual and formalized relationships can provide. He will never relax in Brittles's company, even when invited to, as when his advice is sought or he is offered a "chaw" of tobacco. He remains alone, committed to the lost cause of the Civil War. He does not consider himself a part of "the Yankee Cavalry," and he works for it in an almost independent capacity. As with Brittles, a lost past is all that has value for him.

Although the narration and dialogue attempt to evoke the traditional value of the cavalry that was present in *Fort Apache, She Wore a Yellow Ribbon* lacks the strong sense of community of the other cavalry pictures. Even as Brittles insists to Quincan-

115

Brittles and Cohill watch Pennell take Miss Dandridge on an ill-fated picnic.

The triangle: Pennell,
Cohill, and Miss Dandridge.

116

Sergeant Quincannon reviewing the troops.

Brittles and Tyree: both solitary individuals.

The corrupt sutler Rynders selling rifles to the Indians.

Sergeant Tyree: the loner.

The cavalry officers.

119

non that the cavalry will be the same when they are gone, "The old days are gone forever," as Quincannon tells the bartender. There are the formalized scenes of the cavalry leaving the post, singing "The Girl I Left Behind Me" and marching past their families and the monuments of the valley, but there are no personal, friendly scenes of the men together. We do not even know of the men except Quincannon, Tyree, Cohill, and Pennell, and they do not play and fight together as do the men of *Fort Apache* and *Rio Grande*. The rituals are not debased, but as in *Cheyenne Autumn* their significance lies in the past, not in the present and certainly not in the future, which does not even exist in *Cheyenne Autumn* and is of no concern in *She Wore a Yellow Ribbon*.

When Brittles cannot go back to rescue Cohill, and Pennell must go instead, Allshard tells Brittles that the young men must learn to lead. But even though Brittles agrees, we know that there will be no more leaders like Brittles. Even if there could be, they certainly would not be Cohill or Pennell, whose actions—fighting over the girl, disrespect to the fallen Southern general, and baiting each other like fraternity boys—certainly do not portend their greatness as leaders. The turning over of command, unlike in *Fort Apache*, is to lesser men, who are not of the caliber of the former leaders.

In the Indian community as well, Red Shirt does not compare in human qualities with Pony That Walks. The old man who wants peace cannot control his braves, and the cruel Red Shirt has won their loyalty. "Too late, Nathan, too late," is his observation to his old friend, and even though the Indian war is averted, it is too late for Nathan and Pony That Walks, too late for their communities, which will now be led by lesser men.

Quincannon and Brittles: sniffing for whiskey.

Quincannon in Brittles' "store bought suit" that lands him in the guardhouse.

120

Pennell, Miss Dandridge, Brittles, and Cohill. The new leaders cannot measure up to the old.

Brittles and Tyree riding into the hostile Indian camp.

The old leaders: Brittles and Pony That Walks.

The cavalry.

Captain Brittles.

The cavalry.

The past of *She Wore a Yellow Ribbon,* symbolized by a buffalo that we actually see for a moment, is not seen and not known, except in the minds and imaginations of the filmmaker and his audience. The past is not pushed out by something new and coarse that destroys its old values, as it is in *The Man Who Shot Liberty Valance;* it simply ceases to exist. In reality, it never existed; the artificiality of Mary's grave and Trooper Smith's funeral convey its unreal quality.

The action sequences have this same unreal quality. They do not really relate to the story, and they are never really established in terms of terrain and purpose. The action simply builds an energy that fuels the film but gives it no direction. Like the use of sound, which creates a symphonic effect, the action carries the film through sensual impressions, not through the story line.

One of Ford's constant preoccupations is the conflict between a man's serving society and his living his life as an individual. The shift in his attitude (toward a greater value in individualism) could be roughly traced through the chronology of his career, but *She Wore a Yellow Ribbon* is then somewhat misplaced. There is almost no community or civilization repre-

Stampeding the Indians' pony herd and averting war.

sented in this film, except in the imagination of the past, where all values reside. There is no hint of the cavalry making the West safe for white democracy. Even in the awkward narration the Indian war is described as a war against the United States cavalry, not against white settlers building churches and schools and raising families in the wilderness.

The cavalry itself represents no community: families are almost incidental and the creation of a new family (Cohill and Miss Dandridge) carries no metaphorical implications. Indeed, it lessens Cohill's character and credentials for leadership. This absence of a direct correlation between the cavalry's actions and the needs of civilization links *She Wore a Yellow Ribbon* more with films set outside the United States, like *Donovan's Reef* or *Seven Women,* than with the other cavalry pictures.

The greatest force in *She Wore a Yellow Ribbon* is the past, rooted in American mythology. That Ford places the American dream in the past instead of in its usual position in the future of his characters' lives is an indication of his growing disillusionment with that dream and his realization of its unreality. It is as though *She Wore a Yellow Ribbon* mourns Ford's own dream, which never really existed except in his own mind.

124

Brittles, minutes from retirement, watches his plan succeed.

Quincannon, Brittles, Tyree, and Mrs. Allshard.

The individual: Nathan Brittles.

9
WAGONMASTER

CREDITS

Production company, Argosy Pictures. *Director,* John Ford. *Producers,* John Ford, Merian C. Cooper. *Associate producer,* Lowell Farrell. *Script,* Frank S. Nugent, Patrick Ford. *Director of photography,* Bert Glennon. *Second-unit photography,* Archie Stout. *Music,* Richard Hageman; songs: "Wagons West," "Rollin' Shadows in the Dust," "Song of the Wagon Master," "Chuck-a-Walla-Swing," by Stan Jones, sung by the Sons of the Pioneers. *Editor,* Jack Murray. *Assistant editor,* Barbara Ford. *Art director,* James Basevi. *Set decorator,* Joe Kish. *Costumes,* Wes Jeffries (men), Adele Parmentor (women). *Assistant director,* Wingate Smith. *Second-unit director,* Cliff Lyons. *Locations filmed in Monument Valley and Professor Valley, Utah. Released April 22, 1950. Running time,* 86 minutes. *Distributor,* RKO Radio.

CAST

Ben Johnson *(Travis Blue),* Harry Carey, Jr. *(Sandy Owens),* Joanne Dru *(Denver),* Ward Bond *(Elder Wiggs),* Charles Kemper *(Uncle Shiloh Clegg),* Alan Mowbray *(Doctor A. Locksley Hall),* Jane Darwell *(Sister Ledeyard),* Ruth Clifford *(Fleuretty Phyffe),* Russell Simpson *(Adam Perkins),* Kathleen O'Malley *(Prudence Perkins),* James Arness *(Floyd Clegg),* Fred Libby *(Reese Clegg),* Hank Worden *(Luke Clegg),* Mickey Simpson *(Jesse Clegg),* Francis Ford *(Mr. Peachtree),* Cliff Lyons *(sheriff of Crystal City),* Don Summers *(Sam Jenkins),* Movita Castenada *(young Navajo girl),* Jim Thorpe *(Navajo).*

SYNOPSIS:

Two horse traders, Sandy and Travis, meet a group of Mormons going west when they bring their stock to town to sell. The Mormon elder asks Travis to be their wagonmaster. The wagon train comes upon a troupe of traveling show people —an older couple and a young woman, Denver—who are lost and dying in the desert. Despite objections from the Mormons, the Elder agrees to take the show people along with them until they reach the California turnoff.

A family of outlaws, the Cleggs, force the wagon train to guide them west. When the show people leave the train at the

California turnoff, Travis asks Denver to marry him, but she refuses. However, the show people are brought back to the main group by the Cleggs, who do not want anyone knowing their whereabouts. When the Cleggs attempt to block the Mormons' final mountain crossing to their valley, Sandy and Travis "make their play" and kill the Cleggs. In a reprise sequence, the horse traders, the Mormons, and the show people are united.

WAGONMASTER

*W*agonmaster was made between *She Wore a Yellow Ribbon* and *Rio Grande,* and it has much in common with the cavalry pictures. The unit in *Wagonmaster* is the Mormon community instead of the cavalry, and the main character, Travis, is outside that community through most of the film. Although Travis may not quite anticipate Ethan Edwards, in the sense that he cannot ever be a part of that community, he does begin to anticipate Ford's later hero who is alienated from the social unit, as in *The Horse Soldiers, Two Rode Together, The Man Who Shot Liberty Valance,* and many non-Westerns including *The Quiet Man* and *The Wings of Eagles.*

The emotional quality of *Wagonmaster* is like that of *Rio Grande* and *She Wore a Yellow Ribbon*—very rich in gentle, nostalgic emotion, underscored by comedy, and not disturbed by any disruption in the eventual integration of all emotional elements into the whole. This deceptively unpretentious film is in many ways the high point of Ford's Westerns. Ford's optimism and pessimism are in perfect balance. The darker side of his vision gives an emotional depth lacking in earlier films like *Stagecoach* and *Drums Along the Mohawk,* but the optimism prevails and renders this film essentially undisturbing and only gentle in its nostalgia, not bitter like the later films.

Wagonmaster has a great deal in common with *Stagecoach.* Both tell stories of a group of people, traveling together, who are menaced by hostile forces that threaten them with destruction. Travis and Ringo are similar types—very gentle and kind, silent but strong willed and capable. Ben Johnson was a minor actor who had worked often for Ford, just as John Wayne at the time of *Stagecoach* was a member of Ford's "stock company." Both are even dressed similarly in black shirts, dark hats, and suspenders. The Dallas character of *Stagecoach* is similar to the Denver character of *Wagonmaster*—a girl with a "shady" background whom the hero nonetheless treats with great respect.

However, *Wagonmaster* lacks the structural problems of *Stagecoach.* The film moves by its own energy, not with the necessities of script. The action sequences, far from working at odds with character development, function as expressions of internal tensions being worked out by the characters. Signifi-

cantly, the Mormons are extricated from a danger far less abstract and alien to them than Indians, not by an equally remote force such as the cavalry, but through their own collective efforts.

The show people function, much as do the doctor and Dallas in *Stagecoach,* as a challenge to the snobbery and complacency of the Mormons. The Mormons' attitude toward them when they encounter them in the desert is certainly not Christian—one young Mormon (who later battles with Sandy over Prudence) is for giving them a wagon and sending them off. He does not want that kind of people in their train. The Mormon women are shown looking dark and clustered, protecting their values from these intruders, and the men only grudgingly agree to give them one of their wagons. Even this "Christian" act is only the Mormons' way of getting rid of them without putting their fates on the Mormons' consciences. It is Travis who insists that the show people go along with them. He calmly insists, and the Elder acts as peacemaker, saying that the Lord had put them here for a purpose, and they had better not interfere with the Lord's plans.

Our own moral assumptions are also held up for us to examine. When we first see the show people, Denver is lounging in her entertainment dress, very drunk and looking very disrespectable in her sexually suggestive pose. Travis is the only one who does not react with moral judgment, even going so far as to offer Denver the drink he thinks she has asked for. Only then do we, and Travis, learn that she wants water, that they are drunk because they have had to drink the "elixir" they sell to keep from dying of

Ben Johnson as Travis and Ward Bond as the Elder in *Wagonmaster.*

The Mormon Community.

"Horse traders:" Travis and Sandy are invited to leave town.

Our first view of Denver: our moral judgements held up for us to examine.

thirst. These show people always maintain a false dignity that sets them apart from the others, even when they are accepted into the wagon train.

Denver is proud and impulsive, a less vulnerable character than Dallas of *Stagecoach*. She walks as though she can take care of herself. At one point she tells Travis to leave her alone, and once, she refers to him as a "rube," but in both instances it is with a fondness that leaves her feelings very open. When he asks her to marry him, she refuses for much the same reason Dallas tries to—she is not his kind, and he will be disappointed when he learns what she really is. Denver runs away, presumably blinded with tears as she falls and picks herself up again without a look back at Travis. She is unsure of her powers of assimilation into the whole, and we are never given any evidence that she can belong to this society. But at the very end, in the reprise shots, she sits happily next to Travis in the wagon, dressed primly for the first time in the film, proving her ability to become one of them.

Denver is at her most charming when she is "little-girlishly" impulsive. When Travis gives her better walking shoes, she first looks around for a dignified way to try them on; then, finding none, she just plops herself on the ground in one decisive movement. She walks the same way, as though once she is committed to a movement, it carries itself through with great energy. We know most of what we do know about her through her way of moving, not through her lines, which tell us only that she is a little aloof and unwillingly interested in Travis. His almost total control responds to this impulsiveness on her part, making them perfectly suited for each other. In the dance scene they whirl together, combining both their movements in an irresistible way.

The Denver-Travis relationship is set off by that between Sandy and Prudence. When Sandy first sees Prudence walking up to the horses with her father, he takes off his hat and bows to her. This action is repeated every time he sees her; even when they are dancing he takes off his hat and bows to her every time she comes around to him in the square dance. Their "romance" is simple and uncomplicated compared to that of Travis and Denver, who have various tensions to work through before they can come to each other. Like many of Ford's memorable lovers (in *Straight Shooting, She Wore a Yellow Ribbon, Rio Grande, The Quiet Man, The Wings of Eagles*), they must work through the problems of the film, which are a reflection of the problems they themselves have internalized, before they can be together. In Ford's most bittersweet stories these problems are too much for the lovers and they never do become a couple *(The Searchers* and *The Man Who Shot Liberty Valance).* As in the cavalry films, the love story is not the most important narrative element, but the eventual union

A darker view of the Mormon community.

of Travis and Denver reflects the resolution of the Mormon community's tensions.

The dance on the fresh-laid boards is the high point of the first half of the film and seems to be an expression of the community's oneness. When we look more closely, however, it is apparent that the four couples dancing the Texas Star (Travis and Denver, Sandy and Prudence, the Elder and the older woman from the show troupe, and Sandy's rival with another girl) represent all the unresolved sexual tensions of the film. The apparent unity is false, easily inter-

Denver "taking care of herself," with Travis' help.

Denver rejecting Travis' proposal of marriage.

rupted and exposed as artificial when the Cleggs walk into the Mormon camp.

Immediately, everything changes. The music stops, the lighting becomes sinister and threatening, the long, secure shots of the busy community give way to frightened and frightening close-ups. The Cleggs are shot individually in close-up with more backlight than front- or sidelight, making them seem even larger and more maniacal. The Elder, Travis, and Sandy are shown in similarly expressive light, making them seem frightened and impotent. The Cleggs have not

As "horse traders" whittle their wood and barter, Sandy grins at Prudence.

Sandy fights over Prudence.

Travis, Sandy, and the Elder.

134

The dance on fresh-laid boards.

When the Cleggs interrupt the dance, the lighting changes and the atmosphere becomes dark and dangerous.

only interrupted the happy community dance, but they have denuded it. Even members of the community are now shot in this high-contrast, isolating style, as if they had had their veneer of civilization stripped from them.

A very few scenes later, this dance is parodied in the Indian dance, which is lighted and shot much like the end of the white dance after the Cleggs have interrupted it. Although the two dances constitute essentially the same ritual for their societies, the Indian dance is far more savage, less melodic, and lacking the grace and movement of the more "civilized" ritual. The white women cluster together in fear during the Indian dance, shot in dark, shadowy light. They are threatened by the dance, and they recede into the background much as they did at the appearance of the Cleggs.

In this caricature of the earlier dance in which its civilized veneer has been stripped away, the sexual tensions of the Mormon community are made explicit. Thus, this dance is also interrupted—by the Indian girl who has been molested by one of the Clegg boys. In the less inhibited society of the Indians, the degenerate, perverted sexuality the Cleggs represent breaks open in a way it could not in the repressed society of the Mormons.

The Clegg boy is bound to a wagonwheel and whipped.

The Indian dance is interrupted by one of the Clegg boys
molesting an Indian girl.

The Cleggs represent perversion brought about by the kind of repression the Mormons practice, and their appearance forces the Mormons to come to terms with that repression.

The first shots in the film are of the Cleggs and their robbery. (In this sequence, the lighting is different from that of the rest of the film until the Cleggs come to the wagon train; it is very high contrast, expressionistically claustrophobic and chaotic.) Then we see the flight of the Cleggs, intercut with shots of Sandy and Travis and the wagon train, linking the journey of the Cleggs' escape closely with the journey of the Mormons. The Cleggs are thus like the Mormons and like the horse traders in being run or edged out of town. (The card player links them in the dialogue when he refers to "Indians, Mormons, show people . . . and horse traders.")

Uncle Shiloh is presumably the boys' father—he refers to them as "my boys" and to Luke as "my oldest boy." But he is called "Uncle," and this perverts the family relationship in both a real and symbolic way. The Mormons also call him Uncle Shiloh, further acknowledging their own relationship to the evil family and making of him a perverted father figure that they must all repudiate before they can cross the mountain.

This is apparent from the Cleggs' intrusion into the community. Uncle Shiloh first takes over a bed, leering at the women and rendering the men impotent. The demand for the Mormons' guns symbolically

Low-key lighting of the pre-credit robbery sequence that introduces the Cleggs.

The Mormons and the Cleggs.

The Mormons.

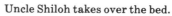

Uncle Shiloh takes over the bed.

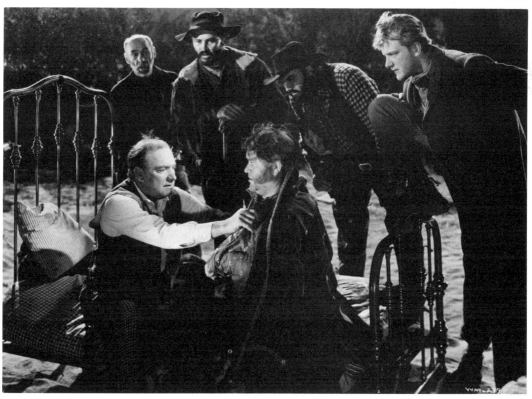

robs them of their virility. The Clegg boys all represent some form of perversion. Floyd carries Denver off repeatedly while Luke voyeuristically leers and laughs maniacally, and Reese lusts after every woman there and eventually rapes the Indian girl. The Cleggs are the physical expression of the Mormons' darker side, much in the same way that the Indians of *Rio Grande* rise up and become a factor as dark tensions enter the world of that film. The Cleggs are what the Mormons must overcome in order to reach their promised land.

The show people also represent eroticism of an unacceptable, though much less perverted, form to the Mormons. They expose the community's prejudice by their very existence and their refusal to be hypocritical. Denver never tries to act prim and proper while she is with them, and the old woman never accepts less than the truth about her nonlegitimatized relationship with the "doctor." And it is Denver's shameless bath that precipitates a fight between Sandy and a Mormon boy over Prudence.

Not until the Mormons have worked through these tensions can they reach their goal. Then they become free from the threat of the Cleggs and incorporate the old show couple into their group. This further frees Travis and Denver from their own isolation, and they, too, become a couple.

Wagonmaster was shot in Monument Valley, but Ford's use of the valley in this film is unlike that in any of his others. The valley does not enclose the world of the film, isolating it within a specific space. This is vital to *Wagonmaster* (and one of its major advantages over *Stagecoach*), because we actually feel that the wagon train is going somewhere. In other films, Ford often uses monuments to limit and block off the horizon. In *Wagonmaster* there is often a very strong diagonal line running straight to the horizon and beyond. In the scene in which Travis and Sandy decide to join the wagon train this line is represented by a fence, extending to the horizon, on which they sit as the wagons pass them. Later, in the climb up the mountain that will be their last obstacle before they actually see their beautiful valley, there is a long-shot of many little wagons making their way up the mountain, over which we cannot see. Their direction is along an unobstructed vertical line, but where it leads remains a mystery to us.

Unrepressed sexuality: Denver.

Sandy, Travis, and the Elder
greet Indians in Monument
Valley.

Sandy, Travis, and the Elder

Both visually and thematically, this mysterious vanishing point of Ford's extended diagonal takes on great significance. We never see the San Juan Valley of the Mormons. We feel the sense of destination through the use of the diagonal line and the lack of self-enclosing terrain, and we see their faces when they look upon it. But this new land exists only in Ford's mind and in theirs, never visually in the film. It remains a dream, more haunting and more emotionally real because of its lack of physical expression.

The last shots are of the journey again, expressing the transcendent unity of those on the wagon train. Now that the Cleggs have been defeated, a unity is possible that could not exist when their presence was poisoning the wagon train and when its own interior tensions were unsettled. The reprise of the journey is not really a reprise; some shots in this sequence did not exist in the body of the film. Sandy and Prudence, Travis and Denver together in wagons, and the elder, Sandy, and Travis singing together—these shots are not in the film, but they belong emotionally in the reprise because they express the emotional unity that now exists.

The showpeople dressed as they appear in the reprise scenes: now a part of the community.

The confrontation between the Cleggs and the Mormons.

The primary drive in *Wagonmaster* is thus toward assimilation, toward a creation of a whole from the various parts of the film. The reprise ending, though confusing in time and space, is right because these shots of all the characters, unified into one harmonious and cohesive community, express perfectly the emotional climax of the film.

The concept of such a reprise leads one to examine the nature of the work itself. If its central purpose were merely to tell a story, falsifying that story in the last scenes would be tantamount to a betrayal of the work. But if the film is the creation of an artistic sensibility in which emotional validity takes precedence over any other concern, the reprise is exactly right. It becomes the reaffirmation of a work whose value lies above all in its power to move people emotionally.

Travis and Denver.

145

10
RIO GRANDE

CREDITS

Production company, Argosy Pictures. *Director,* John Ford. *Producers,* John Ford, Merian C. Cooper. *Script,* James Kevin McGuinness; based on James Warner Bellah's story "MISSION WITH NO RECORD." *Director of photography,* Bert Glennon. *Second-unit photography,* Archie Stout. *Special Effects,* Howard and Theodore Lydecker. *Music,* Victor Young; songs: "My Gal Is Purple," "Footsore Cavalry," "Yellow Stripes," by Stan Jones; "Aha, San Antone," by Dale Evans; "Cattle Call," by Tex Owens; "Erie Canal," "I'll Take You Home Again, Kathleen," "Down by the Glen Side," "You're in the Army Now" sung by the Sons of the Pioneers. *Editor,* Jack Murray. *Assistant editor,* Barbara Ford. *Art director,* Frank Hotaling. *Set decorators,* John McCarthy, Jr., Charles Thompson. *Costumes,* Adele Palmer. *Second-unit director,* Cliff Lyons. *Locations filmed in Monument Valley and Mexican Hat, Utah. Released November 15, 1950. Running time,* 105 minutes. *Distributor,* Republic.

CAST

John Wayne *(Lieutenant Colonel Kirby Yorke)*, Maureen O'Hara *(Kathleen Yorke)*, Ben Johnson *(Trooper Tyree)*, Claude Jarman, Jr. *(Trooper Jeff Yorke)*, Harry Carey, Jr. *(Trooper Daniel "Sandy" Boone)*, Chill Wills *(Doctor Wilkins)*, J. Carroll Naish *(General Philip Sheridan)*, Victor McLaglen *(Sergeant Quincannon)*, Grant Withers *(deputy marshal)*, Peter Ortiz *(Captain St. Jacques)*, Steve Pendleton *(Captain Prescott)*, Karolyn Grimes *(Margaret Mary)*, Alberto Morin *(lieutenant)*, Stan Jones *(sergeant)*, Fred Kennedy *(Heinze)*, Jack Pennick, Pat Wayne, Chuck Roberson; the Sons of the Pioneers *(regimental singers)*: Ken Curtis, Hugh Farr, Karl Farr, Lloyd Perryman, Shug Fisher, Tommy Doss.

SYNOPSIS:

Lieutenant Colonel Kirby Yorke finds his son, Jeff, among his new recruits at his command in the West. Kirby and his wife, Kathleen, have been separated since the Civil War, when in the line of duty as a Northern officer he was required to burn her Southern estate. They meet again for the first time in sixteen years when Kathleen comes to the fort to buy Jeff's obligation, which neither father nor son will allow her to do.

Jeff trains to be a trooper, winning his comrades' respect in a fight, while Kirby observes him from a distance. It becomes obvious how deeply Kirby and Kathleen care for each other as they go through a ritual of courting.

With an Indian uprising, the women and children are sent to a safer fort with an escort, but they are attacked on the way, and the children are captured by Indians. Jeff rides back to the fort for help and then, with two other men, sneaks into the church in which the children are held and prepares for the cavalry attack that will allow them to get the children out. In the attack, Kirby is wounded and Jeff removes the arrow. Back at the fort, Kathleen waits with the other wives for the men to return and, when she finds Kirby on a stretcher, takes his hand and walks with him.

*R*io Grande is an almost balletic story of the relationships among a man and his two loves—his wife and the cavalry. The use of music, both as background and as an active element in the narrative, and of formally composed, expressionistic images convey the emotional resonances of the film in a highly stylized manner.

Like *The Searchers, Rio Grande* has a circular structure with the fort as its focal point. As the cavalry troop returns from a mission, moving toward the fort during the credit sequence and into the gate as the film actually begins, we see first forward movements, moving toward the camera and toward a goal, until the soldiers actually enter the fort, when the camera lets the line of tired, wounded, and dirty men move past it.

Ford's use of camera angles immediately communicates the nobility of the cavalry. They have been through a difficult few days; yet our view of them is a heroic one. The men move past the waiting women, not stopping to greet their wives. Such formal discipline, even when unnecessary, conveys the larger cohesion of the cavalry—when they are part of it, each

Colonel Yorke and his cavalry troop return to the fort.

man becomes something greater than himself alone. Even when they are tired, hungry, and possibly hurt, the cavalry's claim on them is greater than their own needs, and the dignity of the whole lends dignity to each member.

The circular structure is completed when the cavalry returns to the fort in the last scene, but there is now a qualitative change in the characters and their relationships—the problems that were presented both in the plot and in the characters are now resolved.

Kirby Yorke, colonel and leader of the troop, is a variation on the character John Wayne always plays for John Ford—the ambiguous hero with something in his past, either revealed or only hinted at, that gives depth to his present. His past in *Rio Grande* is his marriage, damaged by his own fidelity to his duty.

The enormous emotional appeal of this situation is the result of the impossibility of its successful resolution. When ordered to burn his bride's plantation, Bridesdale, there was no way Kirby could act according to all his principles. He had to choose between his wife and his duty. When a choice is between one's own life and devotion to duty, the decision is not so poignant. A Ford hero's highest duty is always to someone or something other than himself. Devotion to a code (which in *Rio Grande* is military duty) is an even higher value than devotion to another person, because it is more difficult to perform and offers less chance of reward.

The loneliness of leadership is more eloquent in Kirby because throughout *Rio Grande* he is offered an option—the return of the love of his wife, whom he still loves. It is not a decision he can make just once, a test he can pass and be done with, but one with which he must deal again with each new development.

The full force of his loneliness is felt when the troopers are outside the fort (his only home), camped at night. As they sing around the fire, Kirby, who has no place in their circle (isolated by his rank and his own sense of alienation), walks alone by the Rio Grande. As we watch him in long shot, the expanse of the river and surrounding empty land dwarfing him, night falls and further cuts him off from any contact or connection with his own family. There is a close-up of his face, expressing all his suffering and loneliness.

Kathleen Yorke is much like Kirby but in a less tempered way. Jeff observes that she is stubborn and proud, which she accuses Kirby of being. Her loyalties are fierce, but she cannot understand Kirby's. To Kathleen, loyalty is a personal thing, extended through personal relationships. "Special privilege to special born," says Kirby of her, but by misunderstanding the basis for her code of loyalty, he is selling her as short as she does him.

When she wants to help Tyree, it is not because he is special born. She wants to give him all the help at her disposal (which happens to be money, in this case) because he is a friend. She sees Kirby throwing away the highest expression of that kind of one-to-one friendship—their love—to follow an *impersonal* order. One feels that she does not expect anything special of him, but only as much as she would do herself. In this he fails her, for she would never have destroyed their marriage for a larger, impersonal whole, even, one feels, if that whole had been her beloved South.

The great attraction of the character Maureen O'Hara usually plays in a Ford film has this strength at its core. She can give everything to her man and her family, but not to his career. In *The Wings of Eagles,* as in *Rio Grande,* she gives him up rather than compromise herself for his career. In *The Wings of Eagles* we feel that she is right—she has a right to expect more from Spig Wead than she gets, and it is his loss even more than hers that they live most of their lives apart. But in *Rio Grande* this is not the case. Kathleen actualizes herself by understanding the limits of her possibilities and extending herself to them. She grows out of herself toward Kirby by agreeing not to demand of him what he cannot give—fidelity to her feelings over his military duty. Through their shared experiences she comes to understand what his duty means to him.

The tension of distance pervades *Rio Grande.* Kirby and Kathleen are held apart by something deep in each of them. The tension this creates between them whenever they are together is irresistible. In their first meeting after a fifteen-year separation, Kathleen is brushing off the dust of the journey when she sees him. His presence stops her action and freezes her for a moment, just as his view of her stops him midstride. When they touch, it is in the formal gesture of his giving her his arm. The very formality of the gesture is an endistancing one, which adds to the tension of the touch—its actuality only accentuates the distance between them.

Later, in his tent, Kathleen looks into his sleeping area, where his cot lies, his coat upon it. In the same kind of connection made when Martha caresses Ethan's coat in *The Searchers,* Kathleen puts her hand to her belly to resist the temptation to touch it, and thereby touch him. She sets the table and washes his uniform with the care warranted when she knows such gestures are all she can have of him and remain true to her own pride.

When Kirby "comes courting" her in her quarters in the fort, she is already surrounded by two of his men, including the French lieutenant. Kirby looks ridiculous in his white jacket, carrying a bouquet of flowers for his wife. The scene is played for its comedy and perhaps to give Kathleen greater dignity in her own sphere, but the effect is the same as when she is in his tent alone. She will not be trifled with (refusing his joke with the Confederate money) but reaches out to him when he is about to leave. It is when he will put himself in a shaky position (coming courting) that she

John Ford, Maureen O'Hara, and John Wayne on the set of *Rio Grande*.

After fifteen years apart, Kathleen Yorke meets her husband Kirby and his sergeant who burned her home during the Civil War.

Kirby and Kathleen Yorke.

Colonel Yorke and General Sheridan.

Kathleen at the fort with Sergeant Quincannon and Captain St. Jacques.

The loneliness of leadership: Colonel Yorke.

Kirby "courting" his wife Kathleen.

restores him to his rightful position as her husband, even if only for a moment.

The most forceful and unexpected scene between them comes when he returns to his tent at night, tired and off guard, and finding her there, takes her in his arms and kisses her. He has been nothing but genteel to her up to now, giving her his arm, his quarters, his table—all the courtesies a man renders a woman. As long as he can keep up the formal distance between them, seeming not to budge an inch from his ramrod role, she must do the same, but when his real emotion comes through she responds immediately. His leaving at that moment seems harder on her than on him, but in their cautious code of relating to one another, the kiss was as forward a step as he could take. The next one must come from her, and so it does when she asks him to kiss her goodbye.

In remaining at the fort after both Jeff and Kirby have refused to go along with her plan to release Jeff,

New recruits, including Jeff Yorke, Sandy, and Travis, are inspected by Colonel Yorke.

The Indian attack.

she chooses to live Kirby's kind of life for a while. No actual reference is made to her staying; we can believe, as she does, that it is for Jeff. But as the man who first greets her puts it, a trooper's mother has no place at the fort. A colonel's lady does.

Kathleen gets a real taste of her husband's life during an Indian attack while she is on the way to Fort Bliss with the other women and the children. When Kirby comes, she is not standing on the hill with the other wives, aprons blowing in the breeze. This is an image of devotion and constancy in Ford's films, an image Kathleen does not yet fit. Not until later does Kathleen take her place with the women. In the last scene, as the cavalry returns to the fort, she stands with them, anxiously searching the line for her husband and son. When she finds them, she has a choice to make, but by this time we are sure how she will decide. In earlier scenes (notably after she faints

152

Rescuing the children.

Kathleen and Kirby united.

during the Indian attack and regains consciousness when Kirby finds her), when Kathleen, Kirby, and Jeff are together, it has been plain that her connection is with Jeff, not Kirby. In this later scene, however, she first goes to Jeff and stands with him a moment, then looks down at Kirby lying wounded on the stretcher. She leaves Jeff on his own, then takes Kirby's hand and walks with him, never looking back at Jeff.

Travis, Kathleen, Jeff, and Sandy.

Colonel Kirby Yorke and Trooper Jeff Yorke.

Yorke allows a fight "of a personal nature" to continue between his son and another trooper.

The cavalry.

Jeff has perhaps been something of a husband substitute for Kathleen during these fifteen years, and that is the reason for her overprotectiveness. She cannot let go of him because she has no other man to hold on to. There are intimations of this when she goes to Jeff's tent and, when his friends have left, kisses him first on the forehead, then on the tip of the nose, then on the lips. It is of course a tender scene, devoid of the uneasy overtones that would come from a Freudian interpretation. It is enough to say that Jeff is all she had of Kirby until the moment when Kirby and Kathleen can accept each other again, releasing Jeff to finally take his rightful place in the family.

Kirby has obviously felt some rivalry with Jeff before this; Jeff has represented some threat to his peace and security (and perhaps his manhood). After Jeff comes to talk to him in his tent, Kirby measures himself against the point in his tent where Jeff's head has touched, and he is pleased to find himself taller. This is a warm touch, showing a human, vulnerable side of Kirby, rather than an indication that he feels his son a sexual threat. Nonetheless it does perhaps further explore the complexities of the Kathleen-Kirby relationship.

In talking to Jeff, Kirby makes it clear that Jeff is there, not as his son, but as another trooper, from whom he will expect twice what he expects from the others. It is a challenge between rivals, rather than the challenge of a son going through the rites of becoming a man. But when Kirby sees Jeff fall from the horses when riding Roman style, his feelings are nothing but paternal. And they are frustrated by his position; his body (and his heart) move forward to go to his son, but his feet remain where they are, and he is a figure of impotence as he stands awkwardly, unable to do what he wants.

Kirby's growing pride in Jeff is first apparent when Jeff enlists, chooses "my way of life." He does not refer to the boy by name, however, if he can help it, until Jeff has actually done something—brought the word of the attack back to the fort. Later, when he has been wounded and needs Jeff to pull the arrow out, he calls him by his first name, then "son." It is through the act of removing the arrow that they accept each other. As with Martin and Ethan in *The Searchers*, the arrow becomes a physical link between them, removing it is a metaphor for removing the forces that have kept them apart. Kirby wounded is a real person finally, as Jeff has never seen him. And Jeff as a hero is a real person to Kirby. Each approaches the position of the other in that moment, and they become father and son.

Earlier in the film, Jeff's youth (indeed, babyishness) is emphasized. When he is hurt in the fight with the other soldier, he wakes in the hospital with his friends around him and a black eye, looking like a little boy. Kirby looks into the room through a window; his face is framed by the window, and his expression is that of an amused and slightly proud father observing his son going through the first of the "rites of passage" into manhood. The window represents Kirby's physical distance from the boy; it is as though he is observing the childhood he was never a part of, and this is as close as he can get.

In the church Jeff is again photographed with the children to make him look as young and fragile as possible. When Kirby comes he sees Sandy and Travis but looks frantically around for Jeff, who rises somewhat sheepishly with two of the children he came to rescue. It is as though Kirby is shown glimpses of the childhood he never saw, and when Kirby can become the father of the family through Kathleen's acceptance, Jeff can become a young man. Thus Jeff is finally shot in low angle, looking as grown up as Claude Jarman, Jr., can be made to look.

If Jeff is the battleground between Kathleen and Kirby, then Kirby wins in the end. Jeff chooses his father's way of life, to Kathleen's grave displeasure. He refuses her wishes and finally becomes as bound to duty and the cavalry as Kirby is. But his role is more complex than that; rather than the battleground, he is the instrument of peace in first showing them how much they are alike ("... just like him" ..."just like *you* are, Mother") and then providing the circumstances through which they can reveal themselves to each other and be understood. Kathleen is not defeated and relegated to the subservient position of army wife; she comes to love Kirby for the man enriched by tradition and duty that he is. When they entertain the general at dinner and she is asked for a sentiment, Kathleen toasts the cavalry, "my only rival." Through the Indian attack and rescue of the children, the death of one woman, and the wounding of Kirby, she sees what the nature of the cavalry is, something she could never understand when she was part of a South being destroyed.

The general is really the army. He makes no excuses for the role he has played in Kirby's life, acknowledging that though he once destroyed Kirby's home by an order he gave, now he is asking him to put his career in jeopardy by carrying out an illegal but necessary order that can never be acknowledged—to cross the Rio Grande and destroy Natchez. Whether Kirby actually carries out the mission is unclear; the children are taken on the way to Fort Bliss, clearly still United States territory. The town to which they are taken could be in Mexico, but we do not see them cross the river. The question, having been asked and answered ("That's the order I've been waiting for"), is no longer important. It was there only to reassert Kirby's loyalty to his duty.

Rituals and formalized behavior are very important in all Ford's films, especially the Westerns. Kirby's relationships to the military and to Kathleen are expressed ritualistically. In order not to acknowledge but still to experience what is between them emotion-

The Indians hold the white children captive in the church.

The General is the Army.

A formal dinner: Kirby, Kathleen, and the General.

The cavalry post.

ally when they first meet again after fifteen years, Kathleen and Kirby's behavior toward one another becomes one ritual after another—her taking his arm and washing his clothes, their eating dinner together, his treating her with courtly respect.

Music, which functions more profoundly in this film than in any other, deepens and enhances these rituals, as well as the other experiences of *Rio Grande.* When Kirby and Kathleen have eaten together the first evening and the regimental singers come to serenade them, they sing "I'll Take You Home Again Kathleen," obviously a song fraught with meaning for Kirby and Kathleen, since he destroyed her home and now lives in the West. He is embarrassed by it, but she acknowledges that it means a great deal to her, even if it was not of his choosing. This song is

balanced by another that the men sing as they ride, "Yellow Stripes," the most oft-repeated lines of which are, "Kiss your gal and leave her there, /Hope she's going to stay." These songs represent the extreme positions Kirby and Kathleen occupy at the beginning of the film, positions they must both leave to meet each other between.

The song sung for the general, "Down by the Glen Side," expresses love and respect for the general and for the entire cavalry. Such sentiments, through the medium of song, can be expressed without becoming maudlin. These moments occur at night, and they are shot with a formal beauty that liberates them from the usual boundaries placed on emotion and sentiment.

When Kirby goes down by the river alone, the men

156

are around the campfire, softly singing "My Gal Is Purple." Sitting together in a circle around the warmth of the fire, the men sing of a man returning to his wife at night, a wife whom he loves and who completes his life. We feel that Kirby, walking alone in darkness beside the cold water, must be thinking of Kathleen at that moment, and the song only increases the distance between them.

Music is also used gaily, once charmingly, as Kathleen washes clothes to its rhythm, and also in the last scene, when "Dixie" is played and she does a little dance with her parasol, looking slyly at Kirby to make sure he realizes it is "Dixie." The general says the song is for Lee, a generous gesture of respect between two old enemies who are part of a whole that binds them together even when it forces them to kill each other. Of course, the song is also for Kathleen, an admission of the general's part in her unhappiness and an attempt to remedy it.

Ford is fascinated with the Civil War, and he uses it as background in *Rio Grande*. Kathleen is Southern, with all the graciousness, tradition, and pride that implies. With Kirby an officer in the Yankee army, there must always have been great tension between them, even before the burning of Bridesdale, which caused it to become unbearable. Indeed, such tension must always exist in any dramatic context. People and relationships grow stale and uninteresting (to both those involved and those watching) when this tension is lacking.

When that tension is controlled, threatening neither party with destruction, it acts as a catalyst for continued life and rejuvenation. With the burning of Bridesdale, Kathleen was overwhelmed and threatened with destruction if she remained with Kirby; not until Bridesdale is rebuilt do they have another chance, and then only if each is allowed his and her integrity. That Kathleen is given hers, after giving Kirby his by joining the wives when he returns to the fort, is portrayed by the playing of "Dixie" in the final scene. She still keeps her past, different from Kirby's and equally rich. This very difference between them will keep them alive, and the traditions of the South and the military of the North, whose battle almost destroyed what was beautiful about both of them, deepen the meaning. Jeff is the metaphor for the hope of continued life between them, and by growing up, away from Kathleen and toward Kirby, he acts as the agent of their reunion.

Rio Grande is about Kirby and Kathleen, and all other elements are metaphors for what is happening between them. Thus, the Indians in the film exist in their least complex context—they simply represent savage forces, bringing in an element of danger that remains impersonal throughout the film. The Indians therefore remain at the representational level, unlike Scar in *The Searchers* or Cochise in *Fort Apache*. All their actions can be seen as external expressions of

The awards ceremony: the band plays Dixie.

Sergeant Quincannon and Colonel Kirby Yorke.

Kirby's and Kathleen's internal tensions. With the arrival of his wife and son, Kirby's security and safety are threatened, and the Indians attack. They steal the children, including, in an extended sense, his own child, and he must take action to get them back—action that results in his also being reunited with Kathleen.

Rio Grande operates on many levels, the highest being the love story between Kirby and Kathleen and all the others serving to express the complexities of that relationship. Thus, the narrative dilemma (rescu-

157

ing the children), the comedy (derived in large measure from the past of the Civil War), and the other characters (Trooper Tyree, of the South, and, of course, Jeff) all contribute to our understanding of the tensions between Kirby and Kathleen. The external expressions of these tensions are resolved; yet they still underlie the relationship when the film is over, giving it a richness and ambiguity it could not achieve if the elements of the love story had been directly expressed in the narrative.

The first Indian uprising.

11
THE SEARCHERS

CREDITS

Production company, C. V. Whitney Pictures. *Director*, John Ford. *Producer*, C. V. Whitney. *Executive producer*, Merian C. Cooper. *Associate producer*, Patrick Ford. *Script*, Frank S. Nugent; based on Alan LeMay's novel. *Director of photography*, Winton C. Hoch (VistaVision). *Color process*, Technicolor. *Second-unit photography*, Alfred Gilks. *Color consultant*, James Gooch. *Special effects*, George Brown. *Music*, Max Steiner; title song by Stan Jones, sung by the Sons of the Pioneers. *Editor*, Jack Murray. *Art directors*, Frank Hotaling, James Basevi. *Set decorator*, Victor Gangelin. *Costumes*, Frank Beetson (men), Ann Peck (women). *Production supervisor*, Lowell Farrell. *Assistant director*, Wingate Smith. *Locations filmed in Colorado and in Monument Valley and Mexican Hat, Utah. Released May 26, 1956. Running time*, 119 minutes. *Distributor*, Warner Bros.

CAST

John Wayne (*Ethan Edwards*), Jeffrey Hunter (*Martin Pawley*), Vera Miles (*Laurie Jorgensen*), Ward Bond (*Captain Reverend Samuel Clayton*), Natalie Wood (*Debbie Edwards*), John Qualen (*Lars Jorgensen*), Olive Carey (*Mrs. Jorgensen*), Henry Brandon (*Chief Scar*), Ken Curtis (*Charlie McCorry*), Harry Carey, Jr. (*Brad Jorgensen*), Antonio Moreno (*Emilio Figueroa*), Hank Worden (*Mose Harper*), Lana Wood (*Debbie as a child*), Walter Coy (*Aaron Edwards*), Dorothy Jordan (*Martha Edwards*), Pippa Scott (*Lucy Edwards*), Pat Wayne (*Lieutenant Greenhill*), Beulah Archuletta (*Look*), Jack Pennick (*private*), Peter Mamakos (*Futterman*), Cliff Lyons, Billy Cartledge, Chuck Hayward, Slim Hightower, Fred Kennedy, Frank McGrath, Chuck Roberson, Dale van Sickle, Henry Wills, Terry Wilson (*stunt men*), Away Luna, Billy Yellow, Bob Many Mules, Exactly Sonnie Betsuie, Feather Hat, Jr., Harry Black Horse, Jack Tin Horn, Many Mules Son, Percy Shooting Star, Pete Grey Eyes, Pipe Line Begishe, Smile White Sheep (*Comanches*), Mae Marsh, Dan Borzage.

SYNOPSIS:

Ethan Edwards returns home after an unexplained absence of two years following the Civil War. When Captain Clayton

Ethan and the Texas Rangers head out after the cattle rustlers.

of the Texas Rangers comes to ask for volunteers in tracking rustlers who ran off Lars Jorgensen's cattle, Ethan tells his brother Aaron to stay at the ranch with his family and goes in Aaron's place. Forty miles from the ranches they find the cattle slaughtered and realize that it has been a Comanche murder raid.

Ethan and Martin Pawley (a one-eighth-Cherokee boy who was found by Ethan and adopted by Aaron's family when his parents were killed in an Indian massacre) ride back to the ranch, to find it burned and the family dead, except for the two girls, who have been taken captive by the Comanches. After the funeral, they begin on a search for the Indians. Lucy, the older Edwards girl, is found dead, but they do not find Debbie, the younger girl.

Ethan and Martin trail the Indians for five years. When they finally catch up with the Comanche band they find that Debbie, now a grown woman, is one of Scar's wives. Scar knows who they are, and his band attacks them as they camp by the river. Ethan is wounded, and Martin takes care of him as they hide out in a cave. Finally they must return home, just as Laurie Jorgensen (who loves Martin) is about to marry another man. The appearance of Ethan and Martin interrupts the wedding.

A young cavalry lieutenant comes to tell the Ranger captain (who is also the preacher who was to perform the wedding) that Scar's band is camped nearby. In the morning the Rangers move out and attack the camp in the predawn. Martin sneaks in to get Debbie out, fearing that Ethan will kill her now that she has been soiled by Chief Scar. Martin kills Scar and escapes with Debbie. Ethan rides into the tent, scalps the dead Scar, and emerges looking for Debbie. He catches her, lifts her over his head, then holds her as he would a child and takes her home.

As they ride into the Jorgensen ranch, Martin and Laurie, Debbie and the Jorgensens walk into the house, but Ethan stands for a moment outside the door, then turns and walks away.

From its opening scene *The Searchers* is unified on a visual and structural level. The black screen is illuminated by light coming into the dark house when Martha opens the door through which Monument Valley is seen. The house at this angle is between two distant monuments, through which Ethan Edwards is riding toward it. The shot is framed first by the frame of the door, then again by the monuments in the distance, with Ethan a small figure far away in the center of the frame. Our first view looks out upon him from inside, as our last will. He never really belongs inside the house, the society.

Ethan Edwards is perhaps Ford's most ambiguous character. In him are all the qualities that make a Western hero—strength, individualism, self-sufficiency, leadership, authority. He is linked to the small white community by ties of kinship, property (Aaron's ranch), loyalty (his oath to the Confederacy), and duty, but he is never part of that community. With the unanswered questions of Ethan's activities after

Ethan and Martha: repressed emotion.

the war hanging darkly over all the familial scenes, he does not even belong at his brother's ranch.

Ethan does not fit into the rituals of the society. He breaks up the funeral of his brother's family with his impatience to start after the Comanches who murdered them. With everyone gathered around the graves, the reverend praying, and "Shall We Gather at the River" playing in the background, it is visually a formal ritual. The people are set, unmoving, seen from a low angle that looks up toward the reverend. Ethan's physical intrusion into the suspension of the frame is a visual metaphor for his role in the group. He is not bound by its rituals; they mean less to him than vengeance does. As he walks away from the funeral, saying, "Put an amen to it," he represents a movement away from organized ritual, drawing the men away with him. They are wrenched away from their wives and mothers, hastily kissing them as they go to follow Ethan. He leads them from the hill to the horses, from prayer to murderous vengeance.

Ethan interrupts again during the wedding. The community spirit is expressed in the dancing before the ceremony (as in *Drums Along the Mohawk, My Darling Clementine, Fort Apache, Wagonmaster*) and is choreographed into the wedding processional by the reverend. The prominence of women creates a feeling of community, of peace and safety. The men are at their most "civilized" in dress and behavior; even the bar is closed. When Ethan enters the room, the women seem to recede into the background. The men most closely associated with family, like Mr. Jorgensen, who timidly introduces him with "Look Mama, look everybody; look who's here . . ." also recede as Ethan steps up to the bar, which is without question now open. He is joined by the "least civilized" men of the group, those who do not seem "tamed" even in wedding clothes. Again, as in the funeral, Ethan turns the reverend back into the captain.

There is more wildness and savagery in Ethan than in other men who must fight to protect their homes and families. From the very beginning of the journey after the Indians, he is more concerned with vengeance than with rescuing the girls. He wants to rush the Indian encampment when they first see it, which would mean sure death for the children. He reluctantly agrees to the captain's plan of sneaking up on them, but agrees only in terms of a military tactic. And if this order fails (to accomplish Ethan's objective of killing the Indians, not the captain's objective of saving the girls), then "Don't ever give me another."

Ethan is antisocial, and he may be outside the law. Hints are given that he may be wanted, as when he gives his brother newly minted money, with no explanation about where he has been for three years, and when the captain comes to take Aaron and Martin as volunteer rangers to look for Jorgensen's cattle ("You fit a lot of descriptions").

There is a reason for Ethan's antisocial character. From the very first shot, a deep and unfulfilled love is suggested between him and Martha. She is breathless and excited to see him, and when Aaron says, "Ethan?" as they watch him ride in, she looks away from him in what might be shame or unwillingness to share his arrival with her husband. When Ethan kisses her on the forehead, she closes her eyes with restrained emotion. There is a gaiety in her when she ushers him into the house; she sort of swirls around in front of the door before entering and drawing him in behind her.

The clearest hint of this tension is when the captain observes her lovingly stroking Ethan's jacket as she gets it out for him. The captain's reaction—the very careful aversion of his eyes—gives the scene its suggestive power. Every physical touch between the two seems filled with tension and restrained feeling. When Ethan leaves the house after kissing her, her hand remains up, caught in the beginning of a never-completed caress. There is no expression of feeling between Martha and Aaron, or between Ethan and Aaron, and when Aaron asks Ethan why he stayed at the ranch "long after there was any reason," Martha interrupts in what could be an attempt to leave the question unanswered.

For Ethan's part, the first indication of love for Martha comes at the end of the day he has returned to the ranch, while Aaron and Martha are preparing for bed. He goes outside, as though he cannot bear the fact of their marriage, and then looks in through the

Ethan Edwards returns to his brother's ranch.

door frame, to see them close their bedroom door behind them. The implication is that somehow their union makes him an outsider, not only from their house but from society itself.

His feeling is deeply hidden, as evidenced when the men realize that the Indians are probably on a murder raid and that the victims are either Aaron's family or the Jorgensens. Ethan delivers this information with no trace of emotion, and he is contrasted first with Mr. Jorgensen, who breaks down crying, and then with Martin Pawley, who rushes off in blind fear for his family's safety. Ethan stays to cool and feed his horse. He is calm enough to consider that it is forty miles to the ranch, and he will get there faster if he cares for his mount. But as he rubs the sweat off the horse's back, there is an astounding close-up of his face that expresses his anguish far better than the outbursts of the others. Later, when he sees the burning ranch, there is a similar close-up. It is Martha's name he calls as he runs into the havoc of the scene, with no mention of Aaron or the children. And when he comes out of the house after finding Martha's body, he looks absolutely crazed with what he has seen.

The events of The Searchers do not determine Ethan's character; rather, his character determines the events. This is what raises The Searchers far above the level of Stagecoach—the events of the film are expressions of the inner contradictions of the main character. For this reason, Ethan's position outside the family of his brother and the society of the little Western settlement cannot be explained by the unrequited love between him and Martha. That love is determined by the character, and if it has been lost it is because Ethan has always been at his very core outside the pale of society. His character has made the events of his life reflect the outsider position he occupies.

The wild, antisocial aspect of Ethan's character is represented by his affinity with the Indians, especially Scar. Very early in the film, when the men have found the buried Indian who died on the trail, Ethan shows his closeness to their ways when he shoots the Indian's eyes out, so that by Indian religion, he "must

163

The funeral: from prayer to murderous vengeance.

wander forever between the winds." This scene is juxtaposed with the Christian funeral, and it is clear that Ethan is as close to the Indian ritual as to the Christian, perhaps closer. He understands the Indians and knows what their signs mean and what their plans will be. He speaks their language, as Scar speaks his. When they finally meet face to face, it is like one man looking into a mirror. Ethan walks up to Scar, almost touching his nose, and they trade insult for insult. Each knows what the other is, why he is there, and what they must do. In the tent, Scar tells Ethan that Scar's sons are dead and that for each he takes many scalps. In the same way, Ethan wants to kill Indians because Martha (and Aaron) are dead.

Scar is never shown to be as savage as Ethan, except in unseen events, such as the burning of the ranch and the killing of Lucy. But we see Ethan at his worst, when he tries to kill more Indians as they retreat, carrying off their dead and wounded. The other men are shocked at his excess, as they are when he shoots out the eyes of the dead Indian. Ethan's passion is most illuminatingly played against Martin, first when Ethan seems to go mad and kill the buffalo (parallel to Scar's killing the cattle his band ran off the Jorgensen ranch) and later when he wants to kill Debbie. He will wreak destruction even on nature itself to starve the Indians, an act that confuses and appalls Martin. He will do the same thing to his own internal nature—kill Debbie (his kin, therefore part of himself) to exorcise the Indian taint on her.

The action can thus be seen as a manifestation of Ethan's psychological tensions, with which Ethan cannot come to terms in his conscious mind but which he can resolve through their transference into symbolic events. In such an interpretation, Scar becomes the agent of Ethan's unacceptable unconscious desires to invade and destroy the home of Martha and Aaron, from which he feels so excluded, and (presumably) to rape Martha. The close association between Scar and Ethan has its basis here. The Indian's very name may

be an expression of Ethan's rather disfigured psyche. The "search" of the film thus becomes the seeking out and destruction of Ethan's unacceptable desires, and only after Ethan's ritualized mutilation of Scar can he finally accept Debbie.

If in Ethan the forces of savagery and civilization are locked in battle, in Martin Pawley they are peacefully combined. The racial theme of the film is most obvious in his character. In our first view of him he is riding a horse bareback, dressed more like an Indian than at any other time in the movie. There is an immediate link between him and Ethan, for it was Ethan who found him when his parents and their wagon train were destroyed by Indians. Ethan refuses to acknowledge that link. Hostile to the boy from the moment he sees him, he tells him not to call him "uncle" and at every turn denies him kinship.

Martin is one-eighth Cherokee but constantly exhibits behavior more "civilized" than any of the whites. When they are fighting the Comanches at the river, Martin breaks down crying after killing his first Indian, though he is later able to continue the fight.

Martin is still trying to "fetch Debbie home" after even the most civilized influences in the white society (the women) have given her up because she is now a woman grown and "living with a buck." The racism of the white community is not comparable with that of Ethan. The Jorgensens love Martin as their own son, with no second thoughts about his marrying Laurie, and up to a point they want Debbie home again. But a white girl who has been living with an Indian is something different, and we can believe that Laurie's statement that Martha would want Ethan to "put a bullet in her brain" is more than just an attempt to hold Martin at home; it is a reflection of attitudes the entire community holds.

The possibility of unity between the races is expressed in *The Searchers* in the character of Martin Pawley. Even more striking, however, is Debbie's character. Unlike the other white captives, who look so white they are almost albino and who are no longer human because of insanity, Debbie first of all *looks* Indian. When we see her as an adult, she is in Indian costume, which is in no way out of place on her. Her face is dark, and her hair is both the color and style of the other Indian women. This implied assimilation is even more important than Martin's because of the attitude of whites regarding "their women." Women must be kept pure—they carry on the race, so their purity means more than men's. Even though it is clear throughout that Debbie is not really Indian, she does live and sleep with an Indian war chief, and she may have borne his children.

Debbie is assimilated into the Indian tribe to such an extent that the first time Martin says he will take her home she refuses, telling him that these are her people, with whom she wants to stay. Ford's racial

Stalking the Comanches.

Captain Clayton, Ethan and Martha as the Rangers prepare to leave: the Captain averts his eyes from the scene going on behind him.

The homecoming: Ethan and Aaron's family.

An astounding close-up of Ethan as he realizes Martha and his brother's family could be the target of the Comanche murder raid.

Ethan sees the burning ranch.

The Rangers ride to the Edwards' ranch for "volunteers" to hunt for rustlers that drove off Lars Jorgensen's cattle.

Ethan prevents Martin from seeing what the Indians have done to Martha.

Killing Indians: Captain Clayton and Ethan.

Ethan finds Debbie's shawl and doll behind the house.

The captive white girls: crazed by what they have been through.

John Wayne as Ethan Edwards: poised between savagery and civilization.

Wayne, Hunter, Ford, and Bond.

Ford and some Navajos of Monument Valley.

Ford adjusting Pat Wayne's uniform.

Ford showing Jeffery Hunter how to kiss Vera Miles.

167

Searching for Debbie and Lucy:

Brad Jorgensen, Martin, and Ethan go on alone.

Brad, learning of Lucy's death, runs to his death at the Comanche encampment.

Martin returns to the Jorgensen ranch.

attitudes are here made very clear. Debbie's union is juxtaposed with the other "false" marriage, that of Look and Martin. In the white Christian tradition, which has long allowed men to impregnate black slave women but hanged male blacks for looking at a white woman, that union is viewed with humor. From the first misunderstanding (when Martin finds he has bought a wife instead of a blanket), through Ethan's ribbing, to her leaving Martin when he kicks her out of bed, Look provides comedy, not the seriousness of theme that Debbie's and Scar's mixing does. But Look is justified in the end; after her departure, she may have gone back to another tribe or to find information for Martin—we do not know, and it does not really matter. What does is that Martin sees her dead, killed by the U.S. soldiers. We feel with him that there was no need for that—it is as cruel and senseless as it would be for Ethan to kill Debbie.

Other scenes besides the massacre of the Indian village look forward to *Cheyenne Autumn*. When the Indians, including women and childen, are herded in the snow to the post to be locked up, there is little doubt where our sympathies should lie. The last Indian fight is similar. Ethan tells Martin he may get hurt if he tries to get Debbie out before they attack, because "we can't pick our targets." We see many women and children in the village before they attack, and some are deliberately shot down, notably a woman carrying a baby. It is in this scene that Ethan takes Scar's scalp after Martin has killed him, an action more senselessly violent than any we have seen Indians commit.

The fact that Martin and not Ethan kills Scar raises some questions. For one thing, the way in which the killing is done is not believable when one considers that Scar and Ethan have been equated in terms of knowledge, strength, and savagery. Martin is not a fighter, as has been amply demonstrated. The awkwardness with which he kills Scar leads one to believe that there must be a thematic reason for Martin's being the hand that finally conquers the enemy for

Ethan stops Martin from following or preventing Brad from going.

The false marriage: Martin and Look.

whom they have searched five years. Only Martin has a valid reason for killing Scar, and only at that moment. Even the fact that his mother died at Scar's hands is not reason enough, and certainly Ethan's mad vengeance is not. Mrs. Jorgensen warned Ethan that Martha would not want her sons to "waste their lives in vengeance," which is exactly what Ethan has done. Scar cannot be killed for vengeance if the film is to uphold its epic character.

Ethan's coming to terms with Debbie is not accomplished in that epochal moment when he raises her above him. It begins with his acceptance of Martin and the idea of kinship. He becomes fonder and fonder of Martin through the years they ride together, and when they are at the Jorgensen ranch he begins to tell Martin "something"—what, we never learn. He has just assured Martin that he need not continue the journey, since Debbie is no kin to him, and he has mentioned his cattle, which Jorgensen is running with his own. It seems that Ethan is about to offer Martin something—perhaps some form of kinship in the form of property (the cattle) or at least of a better life (with Laurie Jorgensen). Martin cuts Ethan off, and we never know more than what the changed, kinder tone of Ethan's voice has hinted.

It is when Ethan is shot with a poisoned Indian arrow that he really comes to accept Martin. Martin cares for him in the cave (photographed from the inside looking out, as Martha's home was filmed). Martin removes the poison from the wound, a metaphor for removing the poison that has been filling Ethan with consuming hatred. He makes out

The Texas Rangers and U.S. Cavalry massacre the Comanche camp.

Ethan would wreak havoc on nature itself and kill his niece, Debbie, to exorcise the Indian taint on her.

After Martin has removed the poisoned Comanche arrow, Ethan accepts him as heir in his will.

his will, disclaiming Debbie and taking Martin as his heir and, by extension, kin. Kinship then becomes less a matter of blood than of love, or at least comradeship.

With such acceptance as the first step, one could say that Ethan has only one more step to go—the physical rite of ridding himself of hatred, which he does by scalping Scar. But again, such a schematic interpretation robs the character of its depth and ambiguity. Ethan does come to accept Martin and, through love, Debbie. But he never comes to terms with his own essence, which has caused him to be an obsessive character. If such a resolution of interior forces were possible, Ethan could enter the house in the last scene with the rest of his "family." Ethan is bound to "wander forever between the winds," like the Indian whose eyes are gone. He is larger than life, and the demons that pursue him cannot be satisfied through cleansing ritual or social rites.

Lars Jorgensen is in many respects what Henry Nash Smith refers to as the yeoman. He raises cattle and a family, but as in most Ford families, his wife is the strength that keeps things going. Like Aaron Edwards, who says of Martha, "She just wouldn't let a man quit," Lars cannot quit or even show signs of weakening. His wife expresses the populist, Fordian sentiments in her "Texican" speech: that someday this country's going to be a fine place, even if it needs their bones in the ground before that day comes. There is a sense of mission about settling the country. They have lost a son, as well as many of their neighbors, and things may not get any better; but they will never give up. There is no sense that they are there to make money, to be freer than they could be elsewhere, no hint of the reasons that drove the real pioneers out into the West. They are there to make it a better place, a cause worthy of any sacrifice it requires of them.

There is no danger of this desert's being turned into the kind of garden that would make Ford long for the old days. Almost nothing is seen of the men working the land; even their cattle are barely in evidence. The land exists and functions only in a mythical way. There are no plowed fields, herds of beef, or even flowers in a garden. The land is totally neutral, and what will be good about it someday is what the people will bring to it.

Monument Valley is used in nine Ford films, but never so expressively as in this one, in which the deeper meanings of the desert are so much in evidence. It is the only film shot there in which farming or ranching is really an issue, in which people are actually trying to make the desert yield their livelihood. In this context, its indifference to human efforts makes Monument Valley an ideal backdrop against which people try to build something that will be entirely what they make it. The desert does not offer the primitive values of the lush plains, extolled in Walt Whitman's poems—purity, communion with nature, rebirth, and rejuvenation. In Monument Valley all virtues are man-made; there is no help or mercy from the land or from nature, which in its more active form is represented by the Indians.

The grandeur, beauty, and larger-than-life proportions necessary to an epic tale are offered by Monument Valley. Ford uses it as Homer used the sea. It is rather like the sea in its changes, its colors, its moods. Like the sea and unlike lush plains or green mountains, it is resistant to human efforts to shape it, to make it serve them. The most they can do is to match its endurance by refusing to quit, and such perseverance alone is enough to raise them to heroic proportions when a troop of rangers or a line of Indians crosses the screen with the silent monuments behind them. With its immutable timelessness, the valley exorcises men of petty ambitions and individual concerns.

The Jorgensen family often functions to comment on the main characters of the film. The love affair between Laurie and Martin can be seen as similar to the imaginary one between Martha and Ethan, with the woman always waiting and finally giving up hope that the man will ever come home to settle down. At one point Laurie says to Martin, "It's not fair, Martin Pawley. It's not fair and you know it." She is right, but he does not understand as Ethan must have understood when his inaction forced Martha to marry another man. Martha stayed as close to Ethan as she could by marrying his brother, an option that enriches the tragedy of her situation. Laurie has no such option. Laurie and Martin are foils, and their love affair cannot approach the meaning of the one it is standing for. Their relationship serves another and vitally important function—comedy.

Without its rich humor *The Searchers* would be an unbearable tragedy. Lars Jorgensen defines his position in the emotional balance of the film in his very first line when he angrily swears he will raise pigs in the future. When Martin and Ethan come back to the Jorgensen ranch the first time, the antics between Laurie and Martin are light and charming enough to relax some of the tension created by the murders. But no character functions simply as comic relief. Lars has moments of real emotion, as when he realizes that his home may be the one the Indians are going to raid. And later, when discussing Brad's death with Ethan, he says, "Oh, Ethan, this country . . ." with a hopeless gesture that indicates all he has suffered from it.

Charley McCorry functions mainly as comic relief, but he, too, has moments of emotion. When he comes to court Laurie he is a figure of ridicule who makes us feel Laurie's plight all the more. If this is her only option, she may as well risk becoming an old maid by waiting for Martin. But as she looks out the widow after reading the letter, lonely and thinking of Martin, Charley comes up behind her and sings to her, "Gone again, skip to my Lou." He has a beautiful singing voice in contrast to his exaggerated Texican accent, and this lovely song evokes the feeling of home, family, and community. Charley is offering Laurie a real life filled with all that music connotes in a Ford film, while Martin is not even there. So she chooses as Martha chose—to take the option that at least offers her life instead of the death of waiting.

The Jorgensens: welcoming the searchers home.

Comedy: Martin and Laurie.

Martin arrives home just in time to prevent Laurie from marrying another man.

Ward Bond as Captain Rev. Samuel Clayton, John Wayne as Ethan Edwards, and Pat Wayne as Lieutenant Greenhill.

The return of Martin and Ethan at exactly the moment of the wedding prevents Martin from suffering Ethan's fate. Martin always hovers between the antisocial and the civilized, but Laurie provides for him the real link with society without which he would not be able to walk into the house with her in the last scene.

However, his return at this moment points up a weakness in *The Searchers.* The circular form provides an epic structure required for the mythological implications of the Ethan Edwards character and of the story, but the structure becomes labored at this point. The result is that the plot ceases to move by its own power. Ethan and Martin return home for no real reason, and then Scar and his band return to the site of the murder raid five years earlier for no more reason than to complete the circular structure of the film.

The Reverend Captain Samuel Clayton is the last military clergyman in a Ford Western, a tradition carried through *Drums Along the Mohawk,* the cavalry pictures, and many of his non-Westerns. But complex as this combination always is (fighter and religious leader), Clayton is more deeply ambiguous than any of his predecessors. In the first place, he does not function as a chaplain in a military unit; he leads the unit. He does not deplore the violence but justifies it in the ways open to a man of the church. He does not just exist within the military framework; he provides that framework. In him are bound up all the forces antithetical to Ethan — law, organized societal virtues, religious ritual, and duty for a higher purpose. He is the only match for Ethan in the civilized community, with Scar providing that balance in the savage environment.

The implications of such forces within one powerful character are far-reaching, both in terms of his relation to Ethan and in terms of the values he represents. No real moral questions are posed by Clayton's religious or military duties; the purpose of both is the same. Both protect and make it possible for the society to grow, and by combining them in one character, the usual moral question (is killing ever justifiable, even for self-preservation?) is obscured, if not obliterated. The disturbing effect of Clayton's dual identity hints at a basic cynicism inherent in the creation of the character.

Clayton moves between his jobs with no clear demarcation. When we first see him in Aaron's house, he is the captain, come to ask for volunteers. He calls Martha "sister," inquires about Debbie's baptism, and partakes of the hospitality of breakfast and coffee while he is swearing the men in. There is no careful separation of roles, as though they are in no way in conflict. During the fight at the river, he first gives the wounded Nesbie his Bible, saying, "Hold it; it will make you feel better," then goes to kill Indians with a cry of "Hallelujah!" His cry to attack Scar's encampment is, "Let us go amongst them!" And in the wedding scene, he calls for his Bible as a captain would for a gun.

The absence of any moral statement about the reverend captain in *The Searchers* seems evidence that Ford does not want to resolve the dichotomy as neatly as he did in *Drums Along the Mohawk* but intended to leave it ambiguous and disturbing.

The cavalry, a body distinct from the rangers, is clearly and for the first time being held up to ridicule. Most apparent is young Lieutenant Greenhill (who is in command because Colonel Greenhill is his "pappy"), who functions as the blundering butt of the Rangers' jokes. This show of disrespect for the cavalry, which Ford has long ennobled, seems an indication of his disillusionment with values he once held above question. The cavalry's ritualistic nature has been one of its best features, carrying with it emotion and veneration, but in *The Searchers* all honor is with the little band of rangers. The starched, polished cavalry, with its swords and careful organization, is shown as slow, lumbering, and generally a hindrance to the rangers, aside from acting as the cruel arm of an oppressive law in the earlier battle.

Ethan Edwards's odyssey begins with a return to a home that could never be his own and the destruction of that home through forces expressive of Ethan's internal chaos. He works out these tensions as best he can by rebuilding the "family" his alter ego (Scar) has destroyed and by fitting Martin and Laurie into it as surrogates for Martha and himself. But this does not mitigate the driven nature of the character. Ethan is in essence no different when the door closes than he was when it opened; the events that alter men's lives do not touch his.

The return home: Debbie, Ethan, and Martin.

Comedy at the expense of the U.S. Cavalry: the clumsy, over-anxious Lieutenant Greenhill exasperates Captain Clayton.

12
THE HORSE SOLDIERS

CREDITS

Production company, Mirisch Company. *Director,* John Ford. *Producers,* John Lee Mahin, Martin Rackin. *Script,* John Lee Mahin, Martin Rackin; based on Harold Sinclair's novel. *Director of photography,* William H. Clothier. *Color process,* Deluxe. *Special effects,* Auggie Lohman. *Music,* David Buttolph; "I Left My Love" by Stan Jones. *Editor,* Jack Murray, *Art director,* Frank Hotaling. *Set decorator,* Victor Gangelin. *Costumes,* Frank Beetson (men), Ann Peck (women). *Assistant directors,* Wingate Smith, Ray Gosnell, Jr. *Locations filmed in Louisiana and Mississippi. Released June 24, 1959. Running time,* 119 minutes. *Distributor,* United Artists.

CAST

John Wayne *(Colonel John Marlowe),* William Holden *(Major Hank Kendall),* Constance Towers *(Hannah Hunter),* Althea Gibson *(Lukey),* Hoot Gibson *(Brown),* Anna Lee *(Mrs. Buford),* Russell Simpson *(Sheriff Captain Henry Goodboy),* Stan Jones *(General U. S. Grant),* Carleton Young *(Colonel Jonathan Miles),* Basil Ruysdael *(Commandant, Jefferson Military Academy),* Willis Bouchey *(Colonel Phil Secord),* Ken Curtis *(Wilkie),* O. Z. Whithead *("Hoppy" Hopkins),* Judson Pratt *(Sergeant Major Kirby),* Denver Pyle *(Jagger Jo),* Strother Martin *(Virgil),* Hank Worden *(Deacon),* Walter Reed *(Union officer),* Jack Pennick *(Sergeant Major Mitchell),* Fred Graham *(Union soldier),* Chuck Hayward *(Union captain),* Charles Seel *(Newton Station bartender),* Stuart Holmes, Major Sam Harris *(passengers to Newton Station),* Richard Cutting *(General Sherman),* Bing Russell, William Forrest, William Leslie, Bill Henry, Ron Hagherty, Dan Borzage, Fred Kennedy.

SYNOPSIS:

In April 1863 the war is going badly for the Union, and Colonel Marlowe is sent deep into enemy territory to sabotage Confederate supply lines at Newton Station. He takes on Doctor Kendall and a wagon unwillingly, provoking a running

Visual evidence of the glory of the cavalry in
contradiction to the narrative.

battle between the two officers. They stop at Greenbrier for
the night and catch its mistress, Hannah Hunter, listening
through a pipe to their plans. This necessitates taking her and
Lukey, her black maid, along with them.

At Newton Station a Rebel officer—Johnny Miles, former
friend of Kendall's—organizes an attack against the Union
forces, resulting in a massacre of the Confederates. A hospital
for wounded of both sides is set up in the hotel, and as Hannah
nurses the wounded and dying, she watches Marlowe hear a
boy's dying request. As his men destroy the railroad and most
of the town, Marlowe gets drunk and tells Hannah of his wife,
who was killed by doctors, hence his antagonism to Kendall.

As they attempt to return north, the cavalry is caught in a
trap, in which Marlowe is wounded. Kendall treats him and
chooses to remain with the wounded as the rest of the men
escape by blowing up a bridge behind them. Before leaving,
Marlowe tells Hannah he loves her and will be back after the
war.

THE HORSE SOLDIERS

*T*he *Horse Soldiers* is an unusual cavalry picture
for John Ford because the hero is not a career man
and the cavalry does not function as a community
structure. It is Ford's only Civil War film (although
there is a Civil War segment in *How the West Was
Won*), and its setting in the war works against the
usual implications a cavalry-based subject has for
Ford. Since the war is an emergency situation, the
cavalry is not the home of the men who make it up.
What unity it has, Ford imposes on it visually.

The opening shot shows long lines of horses and
men, and such lines become a prominent motif. Thus,
when the men hold a conference under a tree, a
cavalry line moves behind them, and later, when
Marlowe and Kendall are arguing in a field, the line
moves behind them. This line of horses and men
creates a feeling almost in contradiction to the
narrative themes of the film—Ford's compositions

175

John Wayne as Colonel John Marlowe.

evoke the glory of the cavalry, but the narrative portrays the senselessness of war.

The single most important narrative element that contradicts the mythical implications of the cavalry is that Colonel John Marlowe is not an army man by choice. He is as much a draftee as his men, and this removes him from the usual position the leader of the regiment holds in a cavalry picture as the father of the "family." One scene does seem to create a feeling of the community of men. When the officers meet under the tree, Kendall comes late and walks through the camp, stopping to ask directions of the men. One plays a guitar, one washes his face; they seem like a gentle community. But there is more of an anxious feeling of waiting than the feeling of belonging Ford usually creates in such scenes, like the recruit-training scenes in *Fort Apache* and *Rio Grande* or the entire black company in *Sergeant Rutledge.*

The cavalry in *The Horse Soldiers* is a temporary entity. When they first pull out on their mission to Newton Station, they are moving at a good clip and singing "I Left My Love," almost in an echo of earlier Ford cavalry films. As they get tired and begin to slow down, the music slows down with them, and finally they are leading their horses in the late afternoon, tired and dirty, and the music is as slow and ponderous as they are. Ford's use of music and mood are unifying structural and formal devices that make the soldiers a unit, a force that is more than just the men who comprise it. But there is nothing in the narrative of the film to support such a feeling, so it remains in the background, back to earlier and more optimistic films.

The two most honorable and deeply feeling men have these qualities because of fidelity to lives and goals other than the cavalry. The doctor took an earlier oath than his army pledge, and he finally chooses to go to Andersonville prison rather than abandon his men to the clemency of the enemy, because, as he tells Marlowe, "Medicine is where you find it." The nobility of his profession is pointed up not only in his selfless devotion to the wounded, Union and Confederate, but in the scene in the little cabin where a baby is born. He has just lost a man, and now he brings a child into the world; and no matter how often he has done this same thing, he is moved by it. He always wears a white coat, visually separating himself from the other officers and men.

The doctor in Ford's cavalry films is usually comic, often drunken, sometimes wise, but never before *The Horse Soldiers* a truly major character, possibly precisely because a doctor must take a higher oath than to the army. That a doctor occupies the position Kendall does in *The Horse Soldiers* is another indication that Ford is changing his earlier faith in the ability of a military organization to provide its members with a meaning and rationale greater than any individual. Kendall is an individual, isolated from

The officers' conference under the trees.

The officers pose for a portrait.

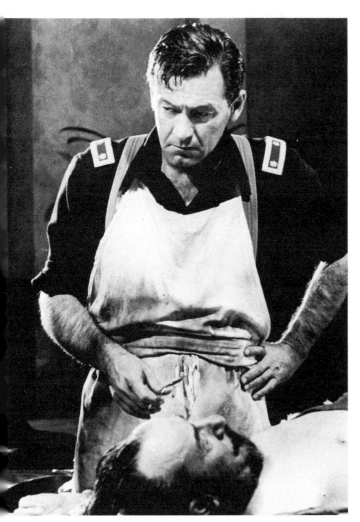

Medicine: a higher oath than to the Army.

the camaraderie of his profession by being in the army and from the camaraderie of the army by being a doctor.

Colonel John Marlowe also has a greater purpose in life than his duty in the army. He is an engineer, a builder who worked his way to the top of his profession in the field, not in the classroom. He is the most ambiguous character in the film, and therefore the most interesting, because he has no easy loyalty, either to the "cause" or to a self-sufficient nobility of profession like Kendall. He is alone, without the family of the cavalry or any other structure to spell out his responsibility in any given situation. He is closest to Ethan Edwards in *The Searchers* in this regard—a lonely, isolated man whose only hope is in personally meaningful action. That he is not nearly so neurotically driven or complex as Ethan Edwards is obvious by the ease with which he finds meaning in his life through Hannah.

The Marlowe character is weakened by the script's easy explanation for the hostility between him and Kendall. In a similar relationship in *The Man Who Shot Liberty Valance,* tension between two characters is only a reflection of their similarity. That is, hostility arises because they are basically alike, and each, in coming to terms with the other, actually comes to terms with the conflicts within himself. This is in many respects what does happen between Marlowe and Kendall, but the story of Marlowe's dead wife (allowed to die senselessly by doctors) and Kendall's later medical treatment of Marlowe lend a superficiality to their relationship. Thus, the use of events as reflections of the characters' internal struggles, which characterizes Ford's best work, is missing here.

177

Kendall remains behind in Confederate territory when the troop moves North.

The northern officers conference in Hannah's home while she spies on them.

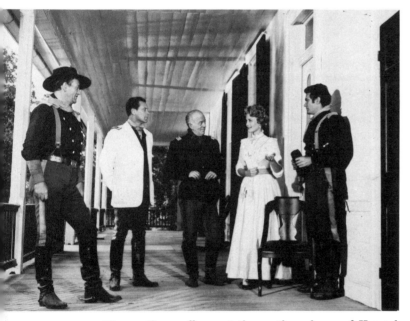

The northern officers at the southern home of Hannah Hunter.

Kendall, excluded from the conference, catches Hannah spying.

Hannah dresses for her own kind of war.

In the clearest expression of a constant Ford theme, the South in *The Horse Soldiers* is represented by Hannah Hunter, a woman, and the North by Marlowe, a man. The people, traditions, and sensibilities of the South are feminine, and those of the North are masculine. This is most interesting, since Ford's sympathies are with the South throughout the film, but his hero is Northern. (This is also the case in *Rio Grande*.)

When the troop first rides into Hannah's plantation of Greenbrier, the men seem as out of place in her yard and walkway as do savages in civilized surroundings. In her house, with its paintings and mirror on the walls, these Union soldiers appear dirty and incapable even of understanding the values represented here. The sergeant looks for a place to spit, and both he and Marlowe breathe a sigh of relief when they are outside again. At dinner, the officers look more groomed, but Hannah is in charge here and remains so until taken over by brute force. Her way of fighting the Yankees is gentle and nonforceful, listening to their plans as she encourages them to think her a scatterbrained, charming bit of fluff. When she is discovered, her rage and anger are expressed in tears. She is helpless against force but powerful in terms of sensitivity and absolute belief in her cause. When forced to ride with them, she represents the entire South with her refusal to give up her dignity or her certainty of victory just because she has no physical power.

Similar is the glory-filled charge of the Rebels at Newton Station. They refuse to allow their military inferiority or the Union's greater numbers to discourage them, and they die in a blaze of glory. The hopeless gesture of Johnny's catching the flag and falling to his knees is as moving as Thursday's joining his men to face certain death in *Fort Apache*.

For Ford, the South has always had the greater glory in the Civil War, both because of its defeat and

Ford showing Constance Towers how to slug John Wayne.

Kendall and southern officer Johnny Miles.

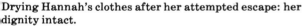

Drying Hannah's clothes after her attempted escape: her dignity intact.

The southern deserters: caricatures of trash.

Marlowe's men intoxicated with the destruction of the town.

The battle of Newton Station: a senseless victory for the North and massacre for the South.

because of its behavior in the face and aftermath of that defeat. The South's preference for death rather than dishonor is the basis of Ford's love. Lost causes are not romantic unless the loser struggles even when there is no hope of success, and that is the South. Hannah perfectly represents this struggle as she is held by force she can never match, calling Marlowe every name she can think of. She tries escaping and every time comes out of it soaked and physically humiliated, but her dignity is intact even when she is dripping and wrapped in a blanket.

Johnny Miles is another such figure whose virtues are in many ways feminine. He has lost an arm, and he is captured, but he still refuses Kendall's friendship. He arranges the attack and is shown through the window of the telegraph house with the train carrying his men reflected in the window glass, the kind of shot Ford reserves for those he loves most—Kirby York in *Fort Apache* and Lincoln in *Cheyenne Autumn*.

The other Southerners in the film are as honorable as Johnny—the sheriff the deserters have captured, the Confederate doctor who aids Kendall in Newton Station, and the Confederate captain who offers Kendall his troop's facilities when Kendall is left by his own troop at the end. Even the bartender in the hotel at Newton Station is the same kind of man—he refuses Marlowe's money, saying he will take care of the wounded without any Union aid.

In one of the most disturbing shots in the film, the Southern women of Newton Station also show their bravery and devotion to their cause. To discordant music, they throw dirt at the Union cavalry as it marches through their streets. This image conflicts with the usual glorified image of the marching cavalry, and as the women hurl insults and dirt at the men, we feel most strongly the wrongness of their mission and of the war.

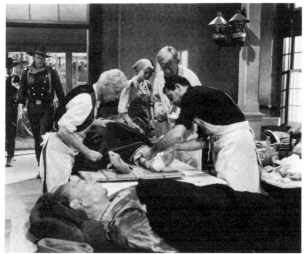

Aftermath of the battle: the hospital.

Marlowe and Kendall prepare to "have it out."

The U.S. Cavalry.

Marlowe and Hannah Hunter.

Kendall and Hannah Hunter.

The war itself is shown to be senseless. John Marlowe goes through increasing disillusionment with the war, his part in it, and his men. Much of this is caused by Colonel Secord, who has political aspirations when the war is over. Everything Secord does or says comes from his concern for his political future or from his cowardice. From the first conference under the trees, when he enthusiastically poses for a picture, Secord's ambitions rise in direct relation to Marlowe's successes. By the final charge he is thinking of the presidency.

Ford has never shown much respect for politicians in his Westerns, but nowhere do we find one so odious as Secord. He is trying only to use the cavalry, his fellowmen, and the war for his own political advancement; yet he has a high rank in the regiment. Never before in Ford's Westerns has such a scoundrel and a politician been allowed to rise so high.

The incident with the deserters is another blow to Marlowe's belief in his cause. Having to deal with such scum, especially with Hannah looking on, is scarcely worth the information he gets, even with the added enjoyment of knocking them flat. The march into Newton Station with the women throwing dirt is but a prelude to the most difficult moments for Marlowe, in the town and in the hospital.

As his men burn the town, they take a fiendish delight in it and, in a few shots, evoke the savage Indians of earlier films. Two mounted men whoop and yell around two burning boxcars in a scene reminicent of the drunken Indians in *Drums Along the Mohawk.* Later, fire seems to engulf the whole place, and Marlowe's men enjoy every minute of it. One comes riding his horse into the saloon, drunk with excitement or liquor or both. Secord runs in to praise the destruction of the railroad line, which in peacetime Marlowe makes his living building. The destruction appalls Marlowe, both in the town and later in the hospital.

The fight over Newton Station (a total victory for the Union forces) is a massacre that Marlowe tried to avoid. He gives the command to shoot at the last possible moment, and he cannot bring himself to watch the Rebel forces crumble on the street as they are caught between the fire from both sides. He almost cries as he exclaims that he didn't want a fight.

In the hospital Marlowe holds a young boy while the lad dies. Feeling all the responsibility for his soldiers, Marlowe goes out to get drunk. They pour buckets of blood out of the hospital, and Marlowe seems to be the only one besides the doctor (neutral because of his profession), Hannah (Southern), and the Rebels to feel any sorrow at the loss of life and suffering.

The march of the little boys is the most moving, profound expression of the lunacy of war in Ford's work, and perhaps in any movie. The oldest among the boys is barely sixteen and talks with a lisp. Two "men" are scratched from the duty roster because they have mumps, and one is carried off by his mother, who is unwilling to lose the last man in her family. He escapes and runs away to the fight, thinking war is a game that will be fun. The little boys in their sparkling new uniforms and make-believe discipline form a sharp contrast with the tired, dirty, threadbare Union army.

Visually, the boys represent a contradiction. Their ordered lines should represent the power and meaning of the army but only show the stupidity of the whole ritual. In the end a little "prisoner" is turned over and spanked, the ultimate expression of the idiocy of the war. Hannah asks Marlowe, "What are you going to do *now*?" and there is nothing left for him to do but to run away from the absurdity of the situation.

In early Ford films, whether they were about farmers (*Drums Along the Mohawk, The Grapes of Wrath*) or the army (the cavalry trilogy), a strong force of mission generally kept the picture going on a mythical level and enriched the narrative. In *The Horse Soldiers,* this is largely absent. It does not appear in the mission, the war itself, or the cavalry. It is conveyed in the film's visual strength and in the heroic shots of long lines of horses and men, but these shots have no meaning to the narrative. The story carries no thrust, and only the love story moves toward any meaningful conclusion.

The John-Hannah relationship in The *Horse Soldiers* carries many overtones of the Kathleen-Kirby relationship in *Rio Grande*. In each, the woman is of the South and the man is forced to wreak destruction on her land. Each has her or his own base, and they can come together as equals because of their differences. The relationship is not as rich in *The Horse*

The last battle.

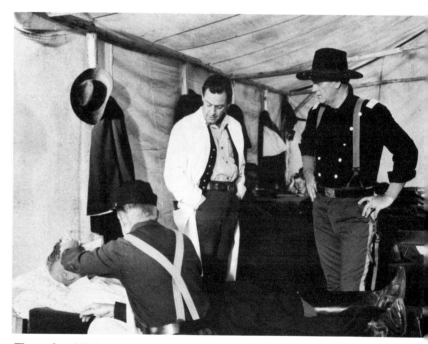
The make-shift hospital.

Marlowe and Hannah.

Soldiers largely because of script weaknesses. Hannah is given explanatory "insight" into John when he gets drunk and tells her about his dead wife—a far more concrete but less meaningful reason for bridging the gap between them than the silent looks they give each other when observing their feelings, as when John momentarily holds Hannah as she stumbles into him after being near exhaustion from working in the hospital, or when Hannah looks at him after he knocks the deserters down.

There is also an echo of the Ethan-Martha relationship of *The Searchers* in the music played in various scenes in *The Horse Soldiers* when Hannah and John meet. One example is when she sits with her two "constant companions" just before the last charge and John walks up to her, his shadow covering her as he comes closer and the two men on either side of her leave the frame. "Martha's theme" from *The Searchers* (which played first when Ethan came home and last when he brought Debbie home) accompanies this image and is heard again when John tells her he loves her, adding much more emotion to the scene than does the awkward script.

The ease with which they fall in love, then part with an easy assurance that they will be together after the war, works against any deep emotional value in the relationship. In Ford's work, the real depth exists because love manages to transcend the tension between people (but not without a struggle). What people go through together, men or women, is the real romance of Ford's loves. An easy love simply cannot be moving, and the love in *The Horse Soldiers* is overexplained and too easily attained.

On the set of *The Horse Soldiers:* John Ford and Hoot Gibson.

Marlowe leaving Hannah and the South.

13
SERGEANT RUTLEDGE

CREDITS

Production company, Ford Productions. *Director,* John Ford. *Producers,* Patrick Ford, Willis Goldbeck. *Script,* Willis Goldbeck, James Warner Bellah. *Director of photography,* Bert Glennon. *Color process,* Technicolor. *Music,* Howard Jackson; song "Captain Buffalo" by Mack David, Jerry Livingston. *Editor,* Jack Murray. *Art director,* Eddie Imazu. *Set decorator,* Frank M. Miller. *Costumes,* Howard Jackson. *Assistant directors,* Russ Saunders, Wingate Smith. *Locations filmed in Monument Valley and Mexican Hat, Utah. Released May 18, 1960. Running time,* 111 minutes. *Working titles:* THE TRIAL OF SERGEANT RUTLEDGE, CAPTAIN BUFFALO. *Distributor,* Warner Bros.

CAST

Jeffery Hunter *(Lieutenant Tom Cantrell),* Constance Towers *(Marcy Beecher),* Woody Strode *(Sergeant Braxton Rutledge),* Billie Burke *(Mrs. Cordelia Fosgate),* Juano Hernandez *(Sergeant Matthew Luke Skidmore),* Willis Bouchey *(Colonel Otis Fosgate),* Carleton Young *(Captain Shattuck),* Judson Pratt *(Lieutenant Mulqueen),* Bill Henry *(Captain Dwyer),* Walter Reed *(Captain MacAfee),* Chuck Hayward *(Captain Dickinson),* Mae Marsh *(Nellie),* Fred Libby *(Chandler Hubble),* Toby Richards *(Lucy Dabney),* Jan Styne *(Chris Hubble),* Cliff Lyons *(Sam Beecher),* Charles Seel *(Doctor Eckner),* Jack Pennick *(sergeant),* Hank Worden *(Laredo),* Chuck Roberson *(juror),* Eva Novak, Estelle Winwood *(spectators),* Shug Fisher *(Mr. Owens).*

SYNOPSIS:

Lieutenant Tom Cantrell is defending Braxton Rutledge, a black soldier of the Ninth Cavalry, against a charge of rape and murder. The story begins in the courtroom and is told in flashbacks, the first being that of Mary Beecher, a young woman returning home to the West after twelve years in the East.

She meets Cantrell on the train that leaves her at Spindle Station, where she is to meet her father. Apaches have jumped

the reservation and killed the stationmaster, whom she finds dead. Rutledge, who is wounded, protects her from the rest of the Indians. In the morning, Cantrell and the Ninth come to arrest Rutledge for the murder of his commanding officer.

Through flashbacks told by Cantrell; the court-martial general's wife, Cordelia; a doctor; Sergeant Skidmore; and Rutledge, the story unfolds. Rutledge and Lucy Dabney were friends, and when she was found raped and strangled, her father (the commanding officer) murdered, and Rutledge unaccountably gone from the post, he was assumed to be the murderer.

On the march to take Rutledge back to the fort, the troop is attacked by Indians, and Rutledge escapes but returns when he sees that his Ninth Cavalry is riding into an Indian trap. His action saves them, but Cantrell must still do his duty by bringing Rutledge back to stand trail.

The prosecuting attorney badgers Rutledge, playing on the racism of the white court. He finally provokes an emotional response from Rutledge, who makes clear his devotion to the Ninth Cavalry. In the final courtroom scene, Cantrell uncovers the real murderer, and Rutledge is cleared. Mary Beecher and Tom Cantrell embrace as the Ninth Cavalry marches by, saluting their thanks to him.

John Ford filmed *Sergeant Rutledge* between *The Horse Soldiers* and *Two Rode Together*. It is a brief respite from his growing disillusionment with values he previously held most dear—the cavalry, sacrifice of the individual, and a legendary story that glorifies a man. He was able to return to these values in *Sergeant Rutledge* because of the special nature of the subject and how these themes functioned in these special circumstances. Thus, Ford could use the black soldier and the black cavalry to represent a group in which the whole still meant more than its individual members and each man contributed to and gained stature from that whole.

Sergeant Braxton Rutledge outside Spindle Station.

As might be expected in Ford's only film about a black hero, the underlying theme is racism, which exists on at least three levels. First is the superficial, obvious racism of Prosecutor Shattuck and Cordelia Fosgate, echoed in the women of the fort and the citizens of the town who want to lynch Rutledge before the trial ever begins. In them is embodied the prejudice that blacks are sexually uncontrollable around a white woman, especially a young, pure white girl.

Cordelia is the most obnoxious representative of this thinking. She and her friends insist on being there for the "spicy" trial and complain loudly when they are put out of the courtroom and again when they must leave while the doctor goes through the "frank details" of the rape and murder. They are intrigued, frightened, and titillated by the sexual nature of the crime and by the black suspect.

In Cordelia's testimony concerning the last time she saw Lucy Dabney, it is evident that her prejudice is sexually based. When she sees Lucy and Rutledge talking, she looks disapprovingly out through the window and speaks a warning to Lucy about being so friendly with him. Lucy is dismayed and puzzled and dismisses the warning as nonsense. In the courtroom, Cordelia cannot even bring herself to point at Rutledge: she refers to him as "... him ..." with a gesture of her little finger. Rutledge is nothing but a dangerous sexual animal to her, and she becomes in caricature the most disgusting representative of this obvious racism.

Prosecutor Shattuck is another representative, or at least user, of this kind of obvious racism. He refers to Rutledge as "this Negro soldier," and later, in his final argument, he refers dramatically to Rutledge as "this man" until he has built up a rhythm, then breaks it by shouting at him, "this *Negro!*" Earlier he has

Cordelia Fosgate and her friends in the courtroom.

Shattuck, Rutledge, and Cantrell in the courtroom.

accused Cantrell of acting like a child when Cantrell insists on giving Rutledge what any white man could expect—every opportunity to be proved innocent. Shattuck constantly tries to emphasize the brutal, savage nature of the crime and impute the same nature to Rutledge. When Mary Beecher tells the first part of her story, he stops her when Rutledge has grabbed her in the darkness and is holding his hand over her mouth. He uses words like "viciously sprang at you ... brutally grabbed you" in an attempt to make Rutledge seem as bestial as possible.

The members of the court exhibit a more subtle form of the same first-level racism. They are surprised and a little put off when the plea is not guilty, demonstrating that they have assumed his guilt before the trial ever got under way. When they go to play cards, Fosgate offhandedly says, "I'm glad to see none of you has mentioned the color of the man's skin."

The next level on which the racism works is more subtle. This is shown in Rutledge's best friends, Mary Beecher and Tom Cantrell. Both are anxious to defend Rutledge and to accuse anyone else of racism; yet their actions show how deeply internalized their own racism is. After Rutledge has saved Mary's life when the Apaches attack them outside the railroad station, he goes into the house to clean up the dead body so it will not offend her. Although she has absolutely no cause for suspicion of him at this point, she watches him through the window with fear and primitive suspicion. When he calls her in, she asks him what he was doing in there, when it is obvious he was doing nothing but cleaning up.

The dim, flickering lights cast a primitive mood over whatever this black man does, and no one knows this as well as he. He tries to get her to go into the other room, but when she won't, he goes about what he needs to do. He asks her for whiskey, which would be a reasonable request from a white man who had been through their ordeal, and she anxiously, suspiciously says, "You want *whiskey?*" Again, she fears the savagery she *knows* is locked inside him.

When she sees that he is wounded, she is immediately suspicious of how he got the wound, even though he has told her the Indians followed him for hours and he fought them off once before. Her irrational fear is evidence of her own latent racism, and perhaps it is at least partially out of guilt that she so vehemently defends Rutledge against both the court and Cantrell.

Cantrell, Rutledge's best white friend, also displays this kind of internalized racism. He knows and respects the soldier Rutledge and, as he later says, thinks there is no better man. That is, he thinks so until very inconclusive evidence causes him to change his opinion almost entirely just because the man is black.

When they ride up to Spindle Station, first thing Tom sees is Mary's hat in the dirt, and he goes directly to his horse to take out the handcuffs. The relationship between these two events is all we need to know about Tom—one look tells him Mary might not be intact, and his immediate reaction is to get the handcuffs to bind Rutledge.

His first words to Mary are, "He didn't hurt you, did he?" after subduing Rutledge like an animal. When Tom talks to Rutledge, Rutledge has the only clear understanding of this racism and refuses to pander to it. When Tom says he wouldn't have believed it, Rutledge says, "You believe it now, don't you, sir?" Tom has Rutledge tied like an animal, and his very strength and beauty make him look even more savage. When Tom tries to accuse Rutledge of playing games, of ignoring their long friendship, and of not being cooperative, Rutledge asks, "What does it all add up to, sir?" What it adds up to is racism, but Tom misunderstands the question and says, "Friendship."

Just as Mary's fanaticism in defending Rutledge might be due to guilt over her racism, Tom's intense desire to be absolutely fair and "go by the book" could be a result of that same guilt. He cannot bear for Mary to accuse him of acting badly toward Rutledge because he knows he has done so (in his mind, if nowhere else), and he does not want to be reminded of it. Rutledge teases him with this, saying, when Tom asks about his wound, "You know what they say about us, sir—we heal fast." If this kind of racism can overpower the best friendship and professional respect, it is so deeply internalized that the most we can do is acknowledge it.

The relationship between Tom Cantrell and Mary Beecher is reminicent of similar relationships in *She Wore a Yellow Ribbon* and *Fort Apache,* in which there is a romance between a woman and a secondary character. The romance is not the major concern, but it reflects the action, and its resolution is intimately tied to the film's resolution. Tom and Mary meet before anyone knows about the crime. They are attracted to each other and plan to see each other again. When next they meet, both know and have reacted to Rutledge, and this is a wedge between them. They clash over his treatment to the extent that Mary undermines Tom's influence with his command, or at least so he feels. It is as though their guilt over their repressed racism must be worked out before they can relate to one another.

Mary was born in the West but has been East for twelve years when she returns to Arizona. She is a little like Miss Dandridge in *She Wore a Yellow Ribbon* because in the beginning she is strong willed, volatile, and not "army." She must learn the value of "the book" and the tradition of command and its function in the cavalry before she and Cantrell can understand each other.

Through the trial, in which she sees Cantrell function objectively rather than subjectively as she has seen him doing, she sees the worth of his values

Spindle Station: Rutledge saves Mary from the Apaches.

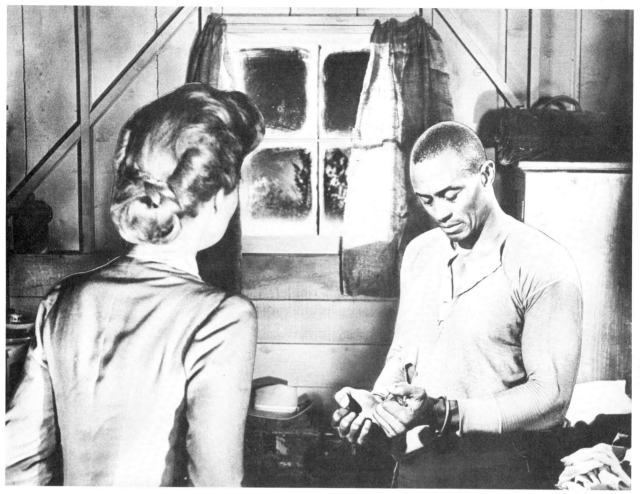

Rutledge is handcuffed by Cantrell, his "best friend."

Cantrell and Mary Beecher: guilt over their own repressed racism.

Mary and Tom in court: their relationship reflects the action of the film.

Mary rushes up to prevent Tom from shooting the escaping Rutledge.

and can apologize for her earlier action. He is hot-headed in the same way Mr. Cohill of *She Wore a Yellow Ribbon* is and picks on her when he has the advantage. Each must come toward the other if they are to get along, and Rutledge is the catalyst by which they do it, just as Nathan Brittles is in *She Wore a Yellow Ribbon.*

The third level on which racism works in this movie is the most subtle, because it exposes the audience's own internalized racism. Ford constantly sets the scenes visually so that we will assume the worst about Rutledge, then learn the truth and have the opportunity to recognize our own racism. We first see Rutledge outside the court when he grabs Mary to keep her from screaming. His black hand on her white throat elicits an emotional response that is not entirely countered by what he is saying. Even after he takes his hand away, it remains poised in front of her throat, and long after there is any rational fear that he will harm her the emotional fear lingers.

Lucy Dabney and Chris Hubble.

Later, when they go inside, Ford shows us the black man taking off his shirt as Mary watches, and again, the irrational fear is conjured up by the visual image. When he asks for whiskey, we do not yet know why he wants it. He lies back on the bed and uncorks the bottle with his teeth, naked to the waist, glistening with sweat, muscles bulging. It is as though Ford is daring us not to be irrationally affected. Whether a viewer would admit it (or even know it consciously), his own internalized racism is being called upon in this scene, and part of what he later responds to in Rutledge is a result of his own guilt at having responded in a racist manner.

Ford understands that racism is internalized in us all, and he knows how to use it so that even while we see characters responding to their own latent racism, we are responding with ours. He also understands the basis of racism, the seat of irrational fears—sex. He used this understanding brilliantly in *The Searchers* and well again in *Two Rode Together,* but in these cases Indians, not blacks, were the focus. In our society, it is far more potentially explosive to deal with the sexual nature of racism with regard to blacks than Indians. From myths about the greater sexual prowess of blacks to fear of their lust for the purity of white women and white women's corresponding thirst for such "degradation," we have all been affected by this disease.

Cordelia unknowingly begins her image of Lucy with a sexual theme. She sees the young girl riding up on her horse and nervously answers her wave. Inside the store, she asks Lucy if it is wise to be riding "astride" a horse. Later, in the court scene when the German doctor tells of discovering and examining the body, he is more angry when he speaks of the "poor little girl" whose purity has been violated than when he speaks of her life that has been taken. He says the rapist-murderer probably took the little gold cross as a "symbol of the purity he had destroyed." This white virginal purity would not mean nearly so much if it had been destroyed by a white man; as the doctor says the emotion-laden words he looks directly at Rutledge.

The structure of *Sergeant Rutledge* is its major weakness. Ford is a very visual director, and his most dialogue-ridden films are generally his least effective. *Sergeant Rutledge* is set primarily in a courtroom, although the flashback technique moves the action outdoors much of the time. The problem is the artificiality of that device. The cutting from flashback to courtroom is generally well done—the action returns to the courtroom for passages of time, to change narrator, or to emphasize and clarify certain points. This structure serves very well to create and sustain suspense, for we know of the crime in bits and pieces before we know all about the circumstances. The technique also serves to nurture the aforementioned audience racism, since it reveals first that there is a crime, then that a black soldier is accused of it, then that it is sexual in nature, without explaining the solution until the very end. Nonetheless, Ford's films are seldom so rigidly controlled in structure, and this heavily theatrical form seems to go against the easy flow usually characteristic of his films.

Ford always introduces comic relief whenever things are getting too serious, but this film is too formally structured to accept comedy as an integral part. All the comedy (except in the very first flashback scene of Mary and Tom on the supply train) occurs in the courtroom scenes involving Colonel Fosgate or his wife. Thus, there is no comedy in the body of the film itself, and we are denied the easy running together of comic and tragic elements that Ford achieves so magnificently in other films.

There are other unsatisfying moments in *Sergeant Rutledge*. Some people have seen it as a racist film, patronizing to blacks and lacking an understanding of the nature of racism. The reason for this may be the last shots of the Ninth Cavalry as it marches by Cantrell and Mary, who have made their peace with each other and are locked in an embrace. The black men march neatly past, every one displaying a large white grin. The impression is both that they share in Tom's winning of Mary by clearing Rutledge, and that they are grateful for his efforts on the part of their "Top Soldier." It is not a successful shot and, appearing in the last scene, leaves the viewer unsatisfied with the conclusion.

Another possible reason why people feel that the film is patronizing is the joking that goes on among the black soldiers, often at the expense of a rookie. But one has only to see any other Ford cavalry film to see that much of the fun and comedy is always at the expense of the green rookies, and to expect him to deny the black cavalry this same kind of camaraderie is to expect a reverse racism characteristic of the liberal consciousness.

The solution of the crime, when Mr. Hubble breaks down and confesses, also does not work entirely successfully. Ford is better at showing things, especially violent or emotional things, or leaving them unsaid and therefore even more powerful (as when Ethan finds Martha and later Lucy in *The Searchers*). Hubble's kind of emotional outburst is not suited to Ford's sensibilities, which are more subtle, and as a result he does not quite know how to handle the scene. Old Mr. Hubble comes off looking like a very poor actor; we do not really believe his motivation for killing the girl. But the real problem here is on the part of the director who has no interaction with the scene or what it is expressing.

The courtroom offers Ford an interior stage upon which to create his own world, just as Monument Valley gives him a self-enclosed world outdoors. He uses both well in *Sergeant Rutledge* and, in fact, links the two visually in the credit sequence. We first see a little wagon driving along in the valley with the monuments behind it. The wagon drives through a gate over which is arched a sign, "U.S. Army Headquarters," and then Cantrell walks along a corridor and through another arch into the courtroom.

The arrangement of the courtroom and the people in it gives Ford the opportunity to structure his compositions with formal control. The table at which the judges sit is in the rear, with five men behind it. The head judge, Fosgate, is in a white coat, and the other four are in black. The witness sits a little to the left and in front of them, with Rutledge balancing this position on the other side. The lawyers balance each other as well, and there are guards at each side of the stage in the foreground. Mary and the doctor often sit on the right side toward the front of the stage, and when it is shot from the back looking toward the front, the guilty Mr. Hubble is framed behind them. In this structure, Ford uses countless three-shot compositions, often with the silent Rutledge at the apex of the triangle, influencing whatever goes on in that scene with his very black presence.

The working title of *Sergeant Rutledge* was *Captain Buffalo*. Captain Buffalo was a legendary character, a black hero who was stronger, braver, and better than

Rutledge and Cantrell.

Mary, Cantrell, and Rutledge on the forced march through Monument Valley.

The courtroom.

ordinary men. Black soldiers were known as buffalo soldiers because of the buffalo hides they wore to keep warm, and Captain Buffalo was their leader. This legendary aspect of the film is very strong. "Captain Buffalo" is the title song, and it is sung when Rutledge stands alone in the night in a low-angle shot, framed against the dark monuments of the valley.

The cavalry and what it means in *Sergeant Rutledge* are thus a little different in substance but not in essence from the other cavalry films. It does represent a greater whole, to which they belong and for which Rutledge would die before bringing its honor into question. And it will continue after any single man has died. But the Ninth Cavalry is also a very immediate, personal freedom for the black men, a freedom they could not achieve elsewhere.

Rutledge orders his men to stop calling him "Top Soldier" and essentially to disown him because the Ninth Cavalry record will speak for them all one day, and he will not allow them to risk it for his friendship. Later, when he talks to Cantrell on the trail, he says that blacks aren't free yet, and in the courtroom he makes a magnificent speech about what his outfit means to him. Shattuck has been badgering him, questioning why he returned to the troop when he had escaped, intimating that he used his bravery (his "stock in trade") in an attempt to gain the court's mercy now. For the first time Rutledge cannot control his emotion, and he rises from the chair, voice straining, and almost breaks into tears as he speaks. He says that he returned because the Ninth Cavalry was his home, his real freedom (as opposed to the freedom he had gained by escaping from Cantrell), and his self-respect. If he ran away, he would be nothing but a swamp-running nigger, "and I'm not that! Do you hear me? I'm a man!"

He rises into heroic low-angle and stands emotionally naked before the racist courtroom. At this moment Rutledge has more dignity in his handcuffs and prison clothes than the rest of the court put together, and they all feel it. Even Shattuck cannot continue his torment of the prisoner and says, "That's all."

Rutledge's statement gains impact from the scene we have just been shown in flashback of Trooper Moffit dying in the battle with the Indians, and Rutledge holding him as he dies. Rutledge tells Moffit that he will have advanced the liberation of his people by giving his little girls a father they can be proud of. The meaning of the cavalry to these men is thus made clear in terms of their families and their futures in a direct way it never could be in other cavalry films.

Cantrell finds the evidence: Lucy's little gold cross.

The Indian attack: Rutledge gives up his freedom to warn the Ninth Cavalry.

It is immediately after this scene in the courtroom that Colonel Fosgate uncomfortably compliments his fellow court members on not having mentioned the color of the man's skin. It is as though he called the card-playing recess to let the overwhelming emotional impact of Moffit's death and Rutledge's speech dissipate.

There is more darkness in *Sergeant Rutledge* than in any previous Ford Western, looking forward to *The Man Who Shot Liberty Valance.* It is night when Mary gets off the train at Spindle Station. The darkness is both an indication of the unknown nature of her future and a foreboding of the danger and fear to come later in the night. With that fear, which contains a sexual element because of Rutledge's blackness, comes a storm that howls and blows outside the station as Mary tries to watch for Indians. In later flashbacks it is also night when the crime is committed and Rutledge flees the fort. Even the daylight scenes have a darker quality to them than early Ford Westerns, particularly the scene in which the young Chris Hubble is found staked out. Even in the immensity of Monument Valley's desert, these scenes have a claustrophobic quality to them.

The last scenes of the film seem very "upbeat" and happy now that the case has been solved and Rutledge absolved, but even these very traditional shots for Ford have that dark quality. The black cavalry is marching in the valley toward the camera, against the backdrop of the monuments. As "The End" title comes on, it frames a line of soldiers marching between it and the Warner Bros. logo, a very Fordian moment. Yet because of the lighting and the deepness of the color, we feel the darker visual style and the somewhat disturbing feeling it elicits even here.

Tom Cantrell and Mary Beecher.

14
TWO RODE TOGETHER

CREDITS

Production company, Shpetner Productions ("A John Ford Production"). *Director,* John Ford. *Producer,* Stan Shpetner. *Script,* Frank Nugent; based on Will Cook's novel COMANCHE CAPTIVES. *Director of photography,* Charles Lawton, Jr. *Color process,* Eastmancolor. *Music,* George Duning. *Editor,* Jack Murray. *Art director,* Robert Peterson. *Set decorator,* James M. Crowe. *Costumes,* Frank Beetson. *Assistant director,* Wingate Smith. *Locations filmed in Southwest Texas. Released July 5, 1961. Running time,* 109 minutes. *Distributor,* Columbia.

CAST

James Stewart *(Guthrie McCabe),* Richard Widmark *(Lieutenant Jim Gary),* Shirley Jones *(Marty Purcell),* Linda Cristal *(Elena de la Madriaga),* Andy Devine *(Sergeant Darius P. Posey),* John McIntire *(Major Frazer),* Paul Birch *(Edward Purcell),* Willis Bouchey *(Harry J. Wringle),* Henry Brandon *(Quanah Parker),* Harry Carey, Jr. *(Ortho Clegg),* Ken Curtis *(Greely Clegg),* Olive Carey *(Abby Frazer),* Chet Douglas *(Ward Corbey),* Annelle Hayes *(Belle Aragon),* David Kent *(Running Wolf),* Anna Lee *(Mrs. Malaprop),* Jeanette Nolan *(Mrs. McCandless),* John Qualen *(Ole Knudsen),* Fred Rainey *(Henry Clegg),* Woody Strode *(Stone Calf),* O. Z. Whitehead *(Lieutenant Chase),* Cliff Lyons *(William McCandless),* Mae Marsh *(Hannah Clegg),* Frank Baker *(Captain Malaprop),* Ruth Clifford *(woman),* Ted Knight *(Lieutenant Upton),* Major Sam Harris *(post doctor),* Jack Pennick *(sergeant),* Chuck Roberson *(Comanche),* Dan Borzage, Bill Henry, Chuck Hayward, Edward Brophy.

SYNOPSIS:

Guthrie McCabe, a corrupt sheriff, is asked by Lieutenant Gary to aid the army in the rescue of white captives from Comanches. McCabe seems a cynical, hard man as he demands $500 for each captive he should recover, but the source of his bitterness becomes clear when they ride into Quanah Parker's camp and find a white girl with Indian

198

199

out of Ford's myths, which will reach its conclusive personification in Ransom Stoddard (also played by James Stewart) in *The Man Who Shot Liberty Valance.* It is in the lead character that this hollowing-out process is first felt. Since *The Searchers* can be seen as Ethan Edwards's internalized battle with the forces that drive him, he becomes a larger-than-life figure of proportions Guthrie McCabe, in *Two Rode Together,* never achieves (and never attempts).

James Stewart has been used in more different ways by directors than any other actor of his stature. His persona is split at least three ways—the Capra hero, the Hitchcock hero, and the Ford hero. Also, somewhere between the Hitchcock and Ford heroes is the Anthony Mann hero. For Capra, Stewart plays a commonsense Man of the People who can be depended on to come through in any crisis. He is largely uncomplicated, except in *It's a Wonderful Life,* in which a darker side of his character is glimpsed and then relegated in a never-to-be dream world. For Hitchcock, Stewart plays a neurotic, ambiguous, deeply troubled and complicated character. Likewise, in the Anthony Mann Westerns he plays a driven man who must work through his inner torments in the hostile environment of the outdoor West. He suffers physically and psychologically in these films (especially in *The Naked Spur*) and he would seem to have nothing in common with the funny, heartwarming Capra hero.

Common to all his roles, however, is Stewart's need to struggle for what he achieves or simply for what he is. The John Wayne persona is always implacable, and there is never any real struggle in terms of the character's integrity, no hint of weakness of resolve or confusion of values. There are always moments of self-doubt (and audience doubt) about his capabilities, motivations, and inner character, especially in the Hitchcock films, in which dark motives and character defects, even perversions, are suggested. Such struggles become physical in the Mann Westerns, but they act as metaphors for inner battles.

To the Ford films Stewart carries all his past characteristics (as any well-established star does), which Ford then manipulates for his own purposes. In *Two Rode Together* and *Cheyenne Autumn* Stewart is immediately introduced as a cynical, uncommitted, mercenary figure possessing great skill and little moral sense. In *The Man Who Shot Liberty Valance* he begins as idealistic and morally intact, but the realities of life change him into an equivocating figure. He is always a practical hero, unlike Wayne, whose inner being cannot be touched, much less shaped, by the outside world and its pressures. Casting Stewart in *Two Rode Together* immediately robs the film of its moral framework, since Stewart does not carry any with him, and its reconstruction is the work of the film.

Richard Widmark also brings to his Ford roles a

children, an old white woman who will not return because of her shame, and a wild white boy who does not want to return. They trade for the white boy, and as they are leaving they are also given a Spanish captive named Elena, the woman of Stone Calf, who is contending with Quanah over power in the tribe. Lieutenant Gary rides on ahead with the boy, while McCabe and Elena camp for the night, expecting Stone Calf. McCabe kills the Indian, then rides on to the fort with Elena.

There he finds that the wild boy has been caged and will be given to a crazed woman who wants to believe he is her son. When she lets him out of his shackles and he kills her, the entire community lynches him. Before he dies, he hears the music box that had belonged to Marty Purcell's brother, and it is obvious that this savage is indeed her brother. His death releases her from the bondage of guilt she has felt for allowing him to be captured, and she later accepts Lieutenant Gary's marriage proposal.

Elena is the subject of great and unkind curiosity at the fort, where she is mercilessly hounded by the officers' wives until McCabe tells them all what hypocrites they are. When he returns to his town, McCabe finds a new "sheriff" in his place, and he leaves for California with Elena.

*T*wo Rode Together is Ford's first obviously cynical Western. It is almost a remake of *The Searchers* in plot, structure, and thematic concerns. *Two Rode Together* does not have the same epic proportions of *The Searchers;* however, it is far more than a poor attempt to repeat the achievement of the earlier film. *Two Rode Together* represents a deliberate hollowing

Jimmy Stewart as Guthrie McCabe and Richard Widmark as Jim Gary.

Widmark, Ford, and Stewart.

earlier film. The difference in the personae of the actors, however, is a key to the orientation the director has taken toward essentially the same themes. The search in the earlier picture makes sense on all levels—the narrative, the personal odyssey, and the mythological implications of building a civilization in the wilderness. In *Two Rode Together*, however, the search is a mockery from the very beginning, its outcome both tragic and ironic for the captives, the searchers, and the society that put the search in motion.

Structurally *Two Rode Together* might seem to ape *The Searchers* in its circular form. The film opens with loud, rowdy men riding into town, then discovers Stewart sitting in a chair on the veranda of Madame Aragon's saloon, hat pulled over his eyes, possibly asleep, unconcerned about anything outside his own comfort. He is the marshal who should see to the noise and commotion the men are making, but he just sits there relaxed and asleep, with no thought for his town. At the end of the film, Lieutenant Gary rides back into town, and there is the figure on the veranda again, in the same clothes as before, hat pulled over his eyes and apparently asleep. But this time it is the new marshal who has taken over the role McCabe has outgrown. From then on the film is on its own, and the apparent circular structure is revealed to be a hoax. The McCabe character has made a circle but is riding away from it, having "finally found something he wants more than ten percent of."

The relationship between Guthrie McCabe and Lieutenant Jim Gary is a key to the film, as suggested by the title. Neither is the hero; both are strong enough and weak enough in their own ways to fragment audience identification and sympathy. In earlier films (*Wagonmaster, The Searchers*), one character is an obvious foil for the other, and in later films (*Liberty Valance, Donovan's Reef*), each lead is a strong, stable figure within his own sphere and does not overlap onto the other. In *Two Rode Together*, however, the two men embody opposing but nearly equal characteristics. In earlier films these elements could sometimes exist in one character (*My Darling Clementine*), and in later films the split into two is definite and leaves both with strong, positive personalities.

certain weakness, though not of a moral nature. His heart and motivations are in the right place, but his wisdom and capabilities are open to question. He is a lesser hero than either Stewart or Wayne, because he does not have the power to actualize whatever he believes in. In *Two Rode Together* he often occupies the Martin Pawley role of *The Searchers,* in both its comic and catalytic functions.

It might seem, then, that *Two Rode Together* is a lesser *The Searchers,* with counterfeit heroes that cannot give the depth and breadth present in the

Madame Aragon's saloon: all we know of the western town.

Ford and Widmark.

The people of the wagon train welcome McCabe as the hero who will rescue their loved ones held by Indians.

Lieutenant Gary is the army man who will follow his duty even if it should cause him death and dishonor, as when he is "ordered" to desert. The substance of Ford's military man is there, but its essence is not, because the army to which he is devoted is peopled by men like Major Frazer and the officers and wives who torment Elena at the dance. McCabe therefore emerges as a stronger, more dynamic character than Gary, whose naïveté leads him to devote his life to an army unworthy of him.

McCabe, on the other hand, has no allegiance to anything except himself and his ten percent of everything in town. He is cynical, mercenary, charming, and immoral. He has ceased to believe in the now obviously meaningless values represented by the West and the army, so is totally reliant on himself for a code by which to live. Even though it is a cynical code, its very existence in the face of the hollow values around him draws us to him. Also, the cynicism is soon revealed to be a defense against a hostile world— he alone knows what a fool's errand the civilians are on in trying to retrieve their loved ones from the Indians. In spite of the promise of money he tells Mr. Knudsen to give it up when he learns that Knudsen's captive daughter, Freda, is now sixteen. The full understanding of that fact registers only in McCabe; not until he actually sees Freda does Gary realize the senselessness of their search.

His naïve belief in old values makes Gary a lesser character; he does not have the depth of understanding necessary to see things as they are. McCabe's cynicism stems, not from inhumanity, but from

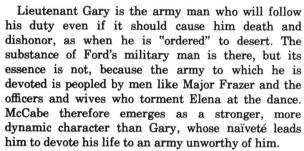

Mr. Knudsen asks McCabe to bring his 16-year old captive daughter Freda home.

having seen too much to have any illusions about righting the world, or even a small part of it. Such a character mirrors Ford's own loss of both innocence and the ability to have faith. In the end, of course, it is McCabe who shows more compassion and faith in people than either Gary or the army officers and their wives.

In earlier films (especially *My Darling Clementine*), the town is a good place where men come together to build schools, churches, raise families and find a better life, much like Walt Whitman's perfect society of the unspoiled West. In *Two Rode Together* the town

202

is Belle's saloon; we see nothing more of it. The town is therefore cut off from the supposed virtues of the West and seems to embody the corrupt pseudo-civilization of the East. This is mirrored in McCabe's clothes. When we first see him he is dressed in Eastern, store-bought clothes that give him a genteel, dishonest look (like his Wyatt Earp in *Cheyenne Autumn*) that reinforces his image as mercenary, self-centered, and isolated from the West. When he goes out on the trail and sheds his superficial air of cynicism and hypocrisy, he also sheds the Eastern clothes and wears traditional Western dress, as Gary takes off his army uniform when he is ordered to desert and accompany McCabe on his "rescue" mission. By this time in Ford's career, in the battle between the values of East and West, the East seems to have taken over the town, and only on the trail, significantly away from any community of men, can McCabe and Gary be natural, Western men.

Until *The Searchers*, the rituals in Ford's films are generally expressive of community spirit; they are at one with the feelings of the hero, who partakes of and is enriched by them. With *The Searchers*, the rituals are to be interrupted by Ethan, but they still carry all their connotations of community feeling and value. In *Two Rode Together*, they seem to have been hollowed out and no longer have the value they should have. They are false, mockeries of former rituals.

As the troop rides through the camp with McCabe, activities are going on as though this were a regular wagon train on its way to build a new community in the West. Yet actually they are just a group brought together because of a common tragedy in their families—loss of a child or wife to the Indians.

The dances, first in the camp when the Clegg brothers fight over Marty, and later, when Elena comes to the cavalry dance, are shells of what dances have been in Ford's movies. They emphasize the lack of depth of the communities they represent. Even the cavalry tradition is represented as shallow, as shown by the major and then by the characters of the officers and their wives at the dance. The major cannot bear to be in the same room with so unspeakable a character as McCabe, who demands money for his work and will put a price on human life. The major asks him to feel for the parents and relatives of those captives and is disgusted by McCabe's indifference to their suffering. Yet by the end of the film, the major not only refuses to pay McCabe what he agreed, but he is grateful to him for having solved the army's problem so nicely—McCabe has got the civilians off the army's back and has done away with the potential troublemaker Stone Calf. The major proves far more reprehensible than McCabe. Not only are his feelings for the people and belief in their cause a sham, but he is capable of using McCabe for his own immoral purposes—breaking the treaty with the Indians.

The dance is one of the bleakest scenes in Ford's

Putting a price on human life: McCabe, Gary, and the Major.

McCabe and Gary trading for captives with Stone Calf.

work. Elena is dressed in light colors. Her hair, which could offer protection in its darkness and abundance, is wrapped around her head, and her very femininity and softness emphasize her vulnerability. As she sits against the wall, she looks even smaller and more helpless because the wall behind her is also light in color and offers her no protection. She is at the mercy of the men who snub her and the women who flit over

Crossing the river.

to ask her embarrassing questions and then flit back to their group to repeat her answers. The usually generous, expansive atmosphere of a Ford dance is funneled into a poisonous, limiting atmosphere in which the one gentle creature there is threatened with destruction. McCabe compares the army community unfavorably with Comanche society, which treated her far less cruelly.

All Ford's Westerns contain an intermingling of the dramatic and the comic that enhances the emotional effect of the positive films and makes the tragedy of the darker ones more bearable. This is also true of *Two Rode Together,* which, without its comedy, would be filled with such despair that it would be unwatchable. But this does not fully account for the role comedy plays in this film, which is the funniest of all of Ford's Westerns. The cynical McCabe plays off the naïve Gary in a clash of values that makes holding any principles seem questionable, then later affirms those principles without darkening the effect of the earlier humor. The film is cynical in both the philosophical and the "worldly" connotations of the word. The sophisticated underplaying of the scene by the river (one medium shot of McCabe and Gary with no cut until Sergeant Posey walks into frame), with its discussion of Belle Aragon's unmistakable refer-

ence to marriage and McCabe's aversion to the idea, has above all an atmosphere of awareness more typical of "sophisticated comedies" than of Westerns.

As in *The Searchers* and *Sergeant Rutledge,* Ford explores the sexual basis of racism in *Two Rode Together.* Hannah Clegg is disgraced because she has been violated by a savage; therefore, she will not return to her family even when the opportunity is offered her. When Mr. Knudsen tells McCabe how old his daughter would be now, we see the first real evidence of suffering in McCabe's face as he tells the father to give her up. The money means nothing to him in comparison with the prospect of bringing home a white girl who has been the instrument of racial mixture and violation. Hannah seems to understand when she is about to leave the Indian camp with them; she suddenly runs away in shame, and Gary finally understands the full implications of their undertaking. He tells McCabe they will leave the girl, and McCabe lashes out that the time to decide that was in the camp before they left. Now they have confronted the sexual racism, and there is no way around it. It is significant that the only captive they choose to bring back is a boy.

Perhaps to permit a more explicit confrontation of racial implications, the character of Elena is some-

204

McCabe and Gary part on the trail back to the army post.

McCabe and Gary.

McCabe and Elena.

what co-opted, first by not being really "white" in a frontier sense (she is a Spanish aristocrat) and second by having an exterior reason for continuing to live with a savage—her religion does not permit suicide. She can then refer to the race pollution more openly, saying that she knows the women of the fort think she is dirty and might soil them.

When Elena is talking to McCabe, she is in medium shot, but when her meaning is explicitly sexual, Ford cuts to long shot, as if to allow her as much privacy and dignity as he can and still explore the subject openly. She does not have children; this also simplifies Elena's return to "civilization," a privilege not granted to Freda Knudsen and Hannah Clegg. This is in some ways unfortunate, for it blunts the racial theme of the film, and even her suggested union with McCabe does not make the point that she is going to be accepted in spite of having slept with a savage. To give her a reason for having committed the most unpardonable sin of all implies that it is a sin and that, had she not been a Catholic, suicide would have been the right course.

When we first see Marty, she is riding a pony bareback. Her hair is in pigtails, and she is wearing a fringed vest. She looks as Indian as a blond girl can, and she continues to wear these clothes until she confronts the savage boy Gary brings back from the Indian camp. That boy turns out to be her brother, of whom she is jealous but about whom she feels tremendous guilt. Her masculine clothes thus take on Freudian overtones—she feels that her father wanted a son more than a daughter and thus assumes the guilt for having lost her brother. She then tries to become the lost son for her father, even to the extent of assuming the Indian dress that he must be wearing, and adopts her brother's music box as the focal point of her obsession. Only after coming face to face with the crazed boy and witnessing his destruction is she freed from the obsession.

The dance: a shell of former dances.

206

McCabe and Elena.

On the trail at night: McCabe and Elena.

Marty and her brother's music box.

The secondary couple: Gary and Marty.

Ford's own racial attitudes are made clear in the captive boy's insistence that he is an Indian and does not want to be "rescued." The boy's feelings question the basic assumption of white superiority. He is not like the women, who feel they have been polluted and cannot return; he *wants* to remain, and he cannot function in a white society that assumes the people he has known as his own are inferior. The director's feelings are made formally explicit when the boy is put in a cage. Ford cuts between a close-up of the boy, seen without the bars obstructing the view, and his point of view of the white people who, shot through the bars, seem to be imprisoned.

In *The Searchers,* the odyssey makes sense in every way as an interior, personal journey and as a rescue mission. In *Two Rode Together* the search is shown to be insane. The women insist on staying with the Indians, and the boy who is taken by force dies for it.

The captive boy: "civilization" kills the "savage."

208

Only the Spanish woman can make the transition, and then only through the love she and McCabe share.

The Indians function superficially in the same way they did in *The Searchers.* Quanah Parker occupies about the same position in relation to McCabe that Scar did to Ethan Edwards, as a kind of alter-ego. Quanah is very different from Scar, but in much the same way McCabe is from Ethan. Quanah is greedy, practical, not entirely the leader in control of his tribe. Following this comparison, characteristics that existed in Scar are split in Quanah just as the usual Ford hero is split between McCabe and Gary. Stone Calf is the other side of Quanah. He is the wild, uncontrollably passionate one, the part of Scar that matches Ethan's savage nature and is exhibited in his killing the buffalo as Scar killed the cattle.

The killing of Stone Calf is remarkably like the killing of Scar. He walks right into view, knowing McCabe must have a weapon, and is killed without resisting. This easy killing makes no sense in narrative terms. So as with the killing of Scar, we must look elsewhere for its rationale. This is found in Elena's story. As she is relating her capture to McCabe, she feels the hysteria and terror of the original event. In a reenactment of the original kidnapping and rape, Stone Calf bursts into their camp just as Elena says, "And then the Comanches came." It is here that McCabe kills him, releasing Elena from her terror.

In the last shots of *Two Rode Together,* McCabe and Elena flee any kind of organized society by escaping into the wilderness. Such an absolutely disillusioned ending is not to be found elsewhere in Ford's Westerns (and is surpassed only in *Seven Women*). No higher values are brought to fruition by men's joining together to create something more enduring than

Re-enacting Elena's capture: Stone Calf is killed by McCabe.

themselves. They can be honorable and at one with nature and their companions only in the absence of structured society. This feeling on the part of Ford has not at this point developed into nostalgia, as it will in *The Man Who Shot Liberty Valance,* or reached for an alternative, even a lost one, as it will in *Cheyenne Autumn.*

Thus, *Two Rode Together* is in many ways Ford's most unredeemed cynical film. It does offer a "new" West (in an unseen California), where people can take refuge and possibly be free again to build something meaningful, but it seems to be through the individual efforts of McCabe and Elena that they will find meaning, not through any building of community values.

Elena waits for McCabe: beginning a new life in California.

Belle Aragon: McCabe has been replaced.

Elena: the mixture of cultures.

15
THE MAN WHO SHOT

CREDITS

Production company, Ford Productions. *Director,* John Ford. *Producer,* Willis Goldbeck. *Script,* Willis Goldbeck, James Warner Bellah. *Story,* Dorothy M. Johnson. *Director of photography,* William H. Clothier. *Music,* Cyril J. Mockridge. *Editor,* Otho Lovering. *Art directors,* Hal Pereira, Eddie Imazu. *Set decorators,* Sam Comer, Darrell Silvera. *Costumes,* Edith Head. *Assistant director,* Wingate Smith. *Released April 11, 1962. Running time,* 122 minutes. *Distributor,* Paramount.

CAST

James Stewart *(Ransom Stoddard),* John Wayne *(Tom Doniphon),* Vera Miles *(Hallie Stoddard),* Lee Marvin *(Liberty Valance),* Edmond O'Brien *(Dutton Peabody),* Andy Devine *(Link Appleyard),* Ken Murray *(Doc Willoughby),* John Carradine *(Starbuckle),* Jeanette Nolan *(Nora Ericson),* John Qualen *(Peter Ericson),* Willis Bouchey *(Jason Tully),* Carleton Young *(Maxwell Scott),* Woody Strode *(Pompey),* Denver Pyle *(Amos Carruthers),* Strother Martin *(Floyd),* Lee Van Cleef *(Reese),* Robert F. Simon *(Handy Strong),* O. Z. Whitehead *(Ben Carruthers),* Paul Birch *(Mayor Winder),* Joseph Hoover *(Hasbrouck),* Jack Pennick *(barman),* Anna Lee *(passenger),* Charles Seel *(president, election council),* Shug Fisher *(drunk),* Earle Hodgins, Stuart Holmes, Dorothy Phillips, Buddy Roosevelt, Gertrude Astor, Eva Novak, Slim Talbot, Monty Montana, Bill Henry, John B. Whiteford, Helen Gibson, Major Sam Harris.

SYNOPSIS:

Senator Ransom Stoddard and his wife, Hallie, return to the Western town of Shinbone for the funeral of Tom Doniphon, the town bum. Reporters ask Stoddard why he came all the way from Washington for this man's funeral, and he tells them in flashback the true story of the man who shot Liberty Valance. . . .

A young, idealistic lawyer, Ransom Stoddard comes West to set up a law office, and his stage is held up as it approaches Shinbone. He is beaten by the outlaw Liberty Valance, who

LIBERTY VALANCE

laughs at his law books as he gives Ranse a lesson in Western law. Tom Doniphon finds Ranse and takes him to Peter Ericson's restaurant to be doctored by Hallie, Tom's girl. Since Ranse has no money, and there is no demand for his professional services, he stays at Peter's as a dishwasher. He hangs up his shingle and starts a school, while remaining a dishwasher. He tries to learn to use a gun, but Tom Doniphon (at Hallie's request) protects him from the violence of Liberty Valance.

The large cattle interests, represented by Liberty, put pressure on the small farmers in the upcoming election to choose representatives for the territorial convention. Tom prevents Liberty from taking over the election, ensuring that Ranse is chosen as one of the representatives. Ranse and Dutton Peabody then publish a story about Valance and his law by power, with the result that Peabody is beaten and Liberty tells everyone that he is gunning for Ranse. Ranse goes out to meet him, is shot in the arm, and with his left hand fires at Liberty, who falls down dead. Hallie embraces him in her relief, and this is observed by Tom, who takes the gesture to mean that Hallie loves Ranse instead of him. He gets drunk and burns down the house he was building for her.

At the territorial convention to elect a governor, Ranse walks out when he realizes that his base of power is the fact that he killed Liberty Valance. Tom stops him by telling him the true story in flashback: Tom fired the shot that killed Liberty. This knowledge allows Ranse to go on to become governor and eventually senator, which we learn when the action returns to the present and Ranse's interview with the paper. The editor, however, decides not to print the story, because "the legend has become fact" and the true story is meaningless. This is echoed as Ranse and Hallie board the train to return to Washington, and the conductor in his efforts to please the senator tells him, "Nothing's too good for the man who shot Liberty Valance."

The themes of *The Man Who Shot Liberty Valance* are those which have concerned Ford from the very beginning of his career—Eastern versus Western values, transforming the desert of the West into a garden, and creating through progress a society in which law and order are not determined by a gun. The film expresses and affirms all these themes; yet at its core is a deep sorrow for the price the town of Shinbone (and America) had to pay. It is Ford's clearest expression of the current of nostalgia and regret that runs through his work, isolated in this film from the compensating forces of the grandeur of the outdoors and the purifying effect of Ford's visual beauty.

The Man Who Shot Liberty Valance was shot almost totally on a sound stage. The few exteriors are bound by fences or buildings (as at the train station when Senator and Mrs. Stoddard are greeted by Link Appleyard). The photography blends foreground with background in a neutral blur. That the filmmaker responsible for the filmic world of Monument Valley, whose most breathtaking scenes are achieved through

inspired use of the landscape, should make a black-and-white film (his first black and white Western since *Rio Grande* in 1950), shot almost exclusively on sound stages, with interior-like exteriors, and filmed mostly at night, is a key to understanding that film. *The Man Who Shot Liberty Valance* is physically the culmination of Ford's darkening personal vision, but the style of the film expresses much more than a darkening of optimism and of Ford's belief in the American dream. The film's visual style lacks more than light: the effect of the darkness is to reduce the mythical proportions of the film, to confine the story within the boundaries of legend rather than to expand it as the beautiful photography of *My Darling Clementine* does. Ford is not presenting a darker legend, he affirms the values of the American dream throughout. What happens in *The Man Who Shot Liberty Valance* is that he expresses the darker dream elements of that legend, and his visual style confines those elements in dream instead of enlarging them into myth.

The first shot shows a train curving through the frame until it comes toward the audience. The effect is that of going inward, of being carried toward an interior story. The last shot shows the train going along a horizontal plane and then out toward the assumed horizon of the frame. It closes the world of the film, shuts it off and ends it instead of opening it up and enlarging its implications for the genre and the American dream, as does the vertical road at the

The first night exterior: filmed on a sound stage.

Senator and Mrs. Stoddard arrive at the train station: the horizon is blocked and limited.

end of *My Darling Clementine*. And just as the very structure of *The Man Who Shot Liberty Valance* confines the legend within flashbacks, so the visual texture limits and isolates the film.

The deep-focus photography creates spatial planes that separate elements in the frame, as in the shot in which Tom Doniphon comes through the door, to see Hallie embracing Ransom Stoddard. Tom is in dark colors, high in the background of the frame, while they are dressed in neutral tones and placed low and in the foreground. The distance between them is on every level—visual, thematic, spiritual, and philosophical.

Chiaroscuro also functions to separate, isolate, and confine. In the little room where Tom Doniphon's plain coffin is laid out, strong areas of light become almost theatrical in effect as Ranse moves in and out of them. Hallie, Link, and Pompey sit in soft darkness, but Ranse stands in harsh light or shadow, removed from their grief, yet not linked with Doniphon. This expresses his ambiguous moral position, his possible contribution to the physical and philosophical meaning of the room, and his power and loneliness.

Ford's often-used contrast of vertical and horizontal lines is expressive in this film in the physical relationship between Ranse and Tom. Ranse first stands very straight and tall, but not strong. He seems held up by a politician's brand of pretensions and appearances. When he looks into Tom's coffin, he stands vertically over the horizontal box. This is immediately contrasted in the flashback with Ranse lying on the ground with Liberty Valance over him— even after he is knocked down once and could conceivably rise, he stays there and in a few moments receives another beating from the upright Liberty. He speaks from this position on the ground and is in the foreground during most of the scene, providing a horizontal contrast to the vertical potency of Liberty Valance.

When he is brought into Peter's restaurant to be doctored, Ranse is put down on a couch over which Tom Doniphon stands, looking down on him. Ranse stays horizontal throughout this scene, standing up only once, with Tom's help. In the scene in the dining room, in which Ranse is tripped while carrying a steak to Tom, he lies on the floor while Liberty and Tom square off on either end of him. Again he offers a horizontal contrast to their vertical strength.

Throughout the film, Ranse seems to possess a collapsible body without real strength comparable to that of Liberty or Tom. He sits on the little couch at Peter's, the camera looking down on him and emphasizing his folded, collapsed form. He walks down the street to meet Liberty in an almost crouched position, and when he must pick up the gun with his left hand he does it by reaching across his body awkwardly, almost falling over with the effort.

Even Hallie looks down on him physically. He seems always to be on that couch when they talk, and during the scene in which she embraces him, she moves a little above him, resting his head on her bosom with her chin on the top of his head. He towers over Tom's coffin only in the first scene, and even then his upright position represents not a real strength, but an assumed one.

Ford makes expressive use of dark and light in the characters' clothing—black and white worn together on the same person connote power, excitement, and vitality. Liberty Valance is the flashiest dresser. His white shirt, black pants, decorated black vest, and silver-handled whip offer more visual contrast than any other character's costuming. Tom Doniphon's dress is a bit less contrasty, with generally dark shirts and a white hat giving way to more solid and dark outfits as the film progresses. Hallie is made neutral through repression by Ranse. At first she wears

Vertical and horizontal positions: defining relationships.

Democracy in action: defeating Liberty Valance's bid for territorial representative.

which is ambiguous from the first shot we see of him in contrast with Tom Doniphon, whose morality is the most constant of any character's. In the scenes of the present (the first and the last in which Ranse is dressed in a white hat and dark suit) his clothes seem a caricature of this expression of consistency, making him appear insincere and dishonest.

The conflicts among the three principal characters parallel the conflicts in Ford's American West. As Hallie and Ranse sit on the train headed back to Washington at the end of the film, she tells her husband, "This used to be a wilderness; now it's a garden. Aren't you proud?" This gives him the responsibility and credit for the change, but we know by now that "credit" might not be the right word. There is a bitterness to her speech and his response that mourns the person and world of Tom Doniphon, which were sacrificed in the building of that garden.

Ranse's gain of power parallels the rise of the power of the law. When he first arrives, his law books are as impotent as he is. Liberty tears out pages and says, "I'll teach you law—*Western* law," as he beats him with his whip. As Tom tells Ranse later, you make your own justice here, and enforce your own law.

As Ranse gains power, the law and its basis—education—become a force in the town. The classroom scene is an archetypal affirmation of Ford's optimistic vision of America—the flag on the wall, the picture of George Washington behind Ranse, and the picture of Abraham Lincoln behind Pompey when he rises to speak. Ranse's speech about the power of the little people and Nora's foreign-accented explanation of how the power structure in a democracy works are at the heart of Ford's vision of America as a place of freedom from oppression and opportunity for all. But even in this scene there are elements of the repression that Ranse's education, law, and order bring with it. He makes Link take off his hat and embarrasses him, tells another man not to smoke, and curbs the spontaneity of the children answering his questions. Hallie's appearance is also repressed by this time, as are her speech and behavior. She is dressed in darker shades than previously, her hair up under a hat instead of free in pigtails.

Hallie's repression is like that of the West—Ranse's influence "tames" her, makes her respectable and educated, but takes the fire, freedom, and passion out of her. In flashbacks she is loud-voiced, expansive, and fervent, but in present scenes she has become soft-spoken and contained. That she goes with Ranse at all instead of with Tom is less a matter of who wins *her* than of who wins the West, and that is determined from the first moment of the film.

As Hallie and the West are repressed by Ranse's "civilization," Ranse is dehumanized by the process. Early in the film he is expressive, subject to outbursts of feeling and easily moved. But by the end this expressiveness has become hollow. When the towns-

generally light colors and is very bright as she radiates around the men, but little by little her bright tones dim.

In the flashbacks Ranse is always dressed in grays, while in present time he wears very contrasty clothes almost in a mockery of their former power significance. He changes clothes throughout the film, but all his tones are neutral. The gray reflects a moral state

Clothing: an indication of power and character.

Democracy in action: electing Ransom Stoddard to congress.

people approach him for a story, he falls into politician's jargon ("mend a few political fences") and an easy, superficial manner that separates him from Hallie, who is so moved by her return to Shinbone. She walks up to Link Appleyard, looking closely at him as though at a dream (as she will look, later in the scene, at Pompey, shading her eyes as though looking a long distance through time at Tom's faithful friend). When she takes Link's hand, they comfort each other by the depth of their feeling for Tom and the past he represents, while Ranse's sympathy leaves Link and Pompey cold.

In the last scene, when Ranse says goodbye to Pompey, the old servant reaches out to him for comfort and receives only slick words of sorrow and a handful of "porkchop money," all that Ranse is capable of giving. When the three old friends sit down by the coffin to mourn Tom, Ranse first walks around, then sits near them, separated from them by the light, then goes out to talk to the newspapermen, as though he has no place in the company of those who feel deeply the loss of Tom Doniphon.

The newspapermen also offer a contrast to Ranse. As the current editor of the Shinbone *Star* comes out to meet the senator, he is buttoning his coat, almost running, and he gives the impression of an

Ranse and the present-day newspapermen: the old values are gone.

The founder and editor of the Shinbone Star, Dutton Peabody, is nearly killed for printing the truth.

insubstantial, temporal personality. Like the cub reporter who has followed Ranse, he is without class or stature. The editor in the flashbacks is a drunk but has real passion, mission, and dignity in him. He has the fire and sincerity the old Ranse Stoddard had but which the senator lacks.

When the editor nearly dies for what he believes, he calls upon our sympathy in a way that emphasizes that Ranse compromised his beliefs. In the way of any successful politician, Ranse has done the possible, the necessary, instead of the ideal. And in spite of the joviality and political jargon, he seems to be aware that in order to gain progress for the West, something of its purity (and his own) had to be sacrificed. For Ranse that sacrifice began with his purchase of a gun and his feeble attempts to learn how to use it. It continued with his allowing his supporters to believe that he shot Liberty Valance. At a crucial point, he could not continue with the thought that his political career was based upon a killing; however, he could allow others to think it.

When he does decide to tell the truth (to the editor of the Shinbone *Star* upon Tom's death) they will not print it, and what might have been a final attempt at honesty with himself comes to nothing. Legend has become fact, so they print the legend. And in truth, Ranse did kill Liberty; in a very real sense his philosophy and dreams for the West killed Liberty, just as they killed Tom.

And Ranse does triumph. His idea of right, law, and progress wins out over the freedom of the old West, and he ends up not only with the future, but also with the girl. The reason for it all is Tom Doniphon, upon whom the spiritual and emotional basis of the film rests.

Ford carefully prepares Tom Doniphon's first appearance with the scenes mythically dominated by his coffin and with the curiosity of the newspapermen, which whets our own. Hallie's obvious feeling for Tom and the restrained emotion between her and Link prepare us for their involvement. The first flashback shows the holdup—a dark, claustrophobic, chaotic scene. It ends with Ranse beaten on the ground, a crazed Liberty Valance standing over him before being dragged away by his men.

The next shot shows the town at night, with Tom Doniphon riding along the street bringing Ranse to Peter's place for care. This scene establishes Tom as a rock of strength, relaxed and totally at one with his world. He rides along to strains of music (the "Genevieve" theme used in *Fort Apache*) that quiet and calm the chaos that has gone before. He is wearing a dark shirt and a white hat, and the contrast links him remotely even at this point with Liberty, but here is calmly assertive.

Tom's progression, from the respectable, capable moral center of the town to a virtual bum, is inversely related to Ranse's progression and in a strange way

Ranse, in his eastern clothes and buckboard, gets a lesson in firearms from Tom Doniphon.

One view of the killing of Liberty Valance.

Pompey saves Tom from the fire he started after "losing" Hallie.

parallels that of Hallie. He is kindly and jovial in the beginning of the film, very much in control and respected by everyone. What he loses (which is reflected in his dress and his voluntary abdication of authority to Ranse) is his personal center. The townspeople still defer first to him and then to Ranse, and he still holds the power that propels Ranse on his way, but he no longer believes he is the center of the town. What he really loses is only Hallie.

Ford's films often have a sexual base to them just beneath the surface—the sexual basis of the racism in *The Searchers* and *Sergeant Rutledge* and the complex Freudian relationships of *Rio Grande, The Quiet Man,* and *The Wings of Eagles.* In *The Man Who Shot Liberty Valance* Tom is in control only as long as he is sure that Hallie is "his girl." When he saves Ranse from Liberty, it is only because Hallie has asked him to. And when he returns to find Hallie cradling Ranse's head, caught in her guilty feeling that she might have

been responsible had he been killed, Tom misinterprets the gesture and thinks he has lost her. The sexual conquest of Hallie is thus meaningful in terms of the American dream and the mythical implications of the story. Hallie represents the country itself, and the struggle between Ranse and Tom over her is the struggle of two ways of life for the future.

But Tom and Ranse do not join equally into either struggle—Tom does not lose either, but decides to give up both.

When Hallie is no longer Tom's, it is because Tom gives her to Ranse, not because Ranse takes her away. Even without Ranse, Tom would not marry Hallie, and the West would not stay free and open. Tom says he is building a room on his house for her, and he burns it down when he sees her with Ranse, but long before this apocalyptic scene there have been hints that Tom will never marry her. When he tells her he is going to go away for three weeks, he looks at Ranse,

224

and Hallie stares at him for a moment while saying goodbye, as if expecting and needing more. He does not respond but turns his back and walks out alone.

Tom's loneliness comes from within him, not from the changing outside world, and the same is true for the West that Ford loves so much. It is doomed to be replaced, not because of the strength of what will replace it, but because of its own nature. Tom represents that West, for which Ford (through Hallie) mourns, but regret is useless, because nothing could have changed the outcome. Progress would have come with or without Ranse.

In this way Tom has a predecessor in Ethan Edwards of *The Searchers*. Ethan does not have Martha, not because he did not ask her first, but because at his core he is a lonely, solitary man who could not settle down on a farm and raise a family. In both films John Wayne plays the mythical hero who is destined to create (in terms of power) the new society but cannot live in it. This sense of sacrifice is very dear to a mythological sensibility and fulfills the ritual need for a man of violence, a hero who is cleansed by his solitude and can never become part of a family or community.

Thus, although the dichotomy of the dream of the West is not resolved, the tensions of the hero, brought into balance, are emotionally satisfying. The hero is a self-sufficient man, a loner who needs no one for his inner sense of completion—the antisocial being we have a part of in our solitary hearts. He lives and dies in the agony of unfulfillment, but our understanding of his suffering purifies us of the need to be solitary and self-fulfilling. He suffers in our place, and the nostalgia we feel for him is tinged with a sense of the sacrifice of our own individuality.

It is the solitary and heroic power of Tom that allows the new society to be built. When Liberty tells Ranse he will teach him Western law and proceeds to beat him, he is teaching him Tom's law of the gun and of force. When Liberty comes into Peter's place and nearly causes a shootout between him and Tom, Tom's cool assurance (and Pompey's rifle) overcome him. When he leaves, Tom jokes, "I wonder what scared him away," and the newspaper editor replies, "The specter of law and order, rising up from the mashed potatoes and gravy." Ranse understands: it is the gun that scared him away.

Over and over Tom must save Ranse, sometimes even physically holding him up, as he does the first night he brings Ranse in. Ranse stands up to make his point about law and almost falls down again, held up by Tom's hand at his shirt. It is Ranse's plan that Tom should serve as delegate to the territorial convention, but Tom refuses and nominates Ranse in his place, assuring his election. He even holds Ranse up when he needs psychological courage—Tom must tell him that he is not responsible for Liberty's death. Tom is, and he is capable of carrying the responsibility for all

Liberty Valance and his men.

he does. Ranse is not, and he continually needs a law or some other justification. The very fact that Tom solves his own problems is justification enough for him.

Almost from the first scene there is a link between Liberty Valance and Tom Doniphon. Ranse observes that Tom is no different from Liberty in his feelings about law and how to deal with problems. The two men of power, one standing for good and one for evil but both deriving their power from the gun, often face off against each other, always narrowly avoiding a showdown. In one case, Ranse prevents the contest. When he is tripped and lies on the floor he rises and picks up the spilled food to keep Liberty and Ranse from shooting each other. Tom dares Liberty eagerly and pushes him to the limit with his taunts and insistence that Liberty pick up his steak. In this scene Tom is as much a provocateur of violence as is Liberty when he shoots up the town and brutalizes people. Later, in the election sequence in the bar, we see another parallel between Liberty and Tom. Both use force, but Tom does so to make sure the right events occur, while Liberty attempts to see that they do not.

The very name "Liberty Valance" would better describe Tom, who stands for personal liberty of a kind that dies with Liberty, and who is valiant beyond any other character. It becomes obvious very early that the two men are bound in a life style. They are not mirror images like Scar and Ethan Edwards in *The Searchers;* they do, however, represent the two sides of the coin that is the old West, with all of its

Making *The Man Who Shot Liberty Valance.*

freedom and passion of the individual. One cannot survive if the other dies; they are bound inextricably in their power-based approach to law, and the only difference between them is moral. Indeed, Liberty Valance is a mythical figure of evil just as Tom is a mythical hero, which explains both his link with Tom and his exaggerated villainy. The last in a long line of totally evil Ford villains (the Cleggs of *Wagonmaster,* the Clantons of *My Darling Clementine*), Liberty sometimes defies belief with his demonstrations of evil. He is as much a representation as Tom is, and he can be destroyed only by his counterpart.

In killing Liberty, Tom is carrying out the last step in his own destruction. He is making the town safe for Ranse, who will succeed him in influence and in directing the town, and he is saving him for Hallie. But these are narrative considerations; actually, Tom is killing himself, destroying a time and a place in which he can function as a whole person. If Liberty is not free to exercise his power wrongly, then Tom cannot be free to exercise his rightly. Tom has saved Ranse before, but never in a way so personally threatening to himself.

The effect is immediately known, as he returns to Peter's and sees Hallie holding Ranse in her arms. In one act of commitment to Ranse's way of life, to the future, he has destroyed himself. His destruction is apparent that very night, as he goes home and burns down what would have been his future—the home he was building for Hallie. From then on, he appears unshaven, uncouth, a wasted image of his former self. Long before he dies he degenerates into a figure largely lacking in dignity and power.

What makes Tom Doniphon such a powerful mythical hero is that he is acting out a ritual. Tom loses Hallie, his future, and his power, not because he chooses to do so out of the goodness of his heart, but because he is enacting the ritual of progress, which destines that the old hero be destroyed so that the new can take his place. A hero of such proportions cannot be defeated by the new, so his fall, born of interior drives and executed consciously and with his full cooperation, carries out the ritual and does not diminish his heroic stature.

The ritual affirms both the social necessities and the mythical hero who had to die with the dream. Any attempt to debunk that hero in favor of the values of the new society would be ineffective in the emotional consciousness of the audience, which needs to share in the ritual. What dies must be of great value to be worthy of sacrifice for the new. This value enhances the new and makes the sacrifice more tragic, but more satisfying as well. Ford's heart, like Hallie's, is with Tom and the old West. And the bittersweet nostalgia at having glimpsed and then lost him for a greater value works in the collective dream that is the history of man and the justification of his evolution.

John Ford in 1961.

Liberty Valance and Doc Willoughby: Liberty pays for his funeral in advance.

16
CHEYENNE AUTUMN

CREDITS

Production company, "A John Ford Bernard Smith Production." *Director,* John Ford. *Producer,* Bernard Smith. *Script,* James R. Webb; based on Mari Sandoz's book. *Director of photography,* William Clothier (Super-Panavision 70). *Color process,* Technicolor. *Music,* Alex North. *Editor,* Otho Lovering. *Sound editor,* Francis E. Stahl. *Art director,* Richard Day. *Set decorator,* Darrell Silvera. *Associate director,* Ray Kellogg. *Assistant directors,* Wingate Smith, Russ Saunders. *Second-unit director,* Ray Kellogg. *Locations filmed in Monument Valley and Moab, Utah. Released December 19, 1964. Running time,* 159 minutes. *Distributor,* Warner Bros.

CAST

Richard Widmark *(Captain Thomas Archer),* Carroll Baker *(Deborah Wright),* James Stewart *(Wyatt Earp),* Edward G. Robinson *(Secretary of the Interior Carl Schurz),* Karl Malden *(Captain Wessels),* Sal Mineo *(Red Shirt),* Dolores Del Rio *(Spanish Woman),* Ricardo Montalban *(Little Wolf),* Gilbert Roland *(Dull Knife),* Arthur Kennedy *(Doc Holliday),* Patrick Wayne *(Second Lieutenant Scott),* Elizabeth Allen *(Guinevere Plantagenet),* John Carradine *(Major Jeff Blair),* Victor Jory *(Tall Tree),* Mike Mazurki *(Top Sergeant Stanislas Wichowsky),* George O'Brien *(Major Branden),* Sean McClory *(Doctor O'Carberry),* Judson Pratt *(Mayor "Dog" Kelly),* Carmen D'Antonio *(Pawnee woman),* Ken Curtis *(Joe),* Walter Baldwin *(Jeremy Wright),* Shug Fisher *(Skinny),* Nancy Hsueh *(Little Bird),* Chuck Roberson *(platoon sergeant),* Harry Carey, Jr. *(Trooper Smith),* Ben Johnson *(Trooper Plumtree),* Jimmy O'Hara *(trooper),* Chuck Hayward *(trooper),* Lee Bradley *(Cheyenne),* Frank Bradley *(Cheyenne),* Walter Reed *(Lieutenant Peterson),* Willis Bouchey *(colonel),* Carleton Young *(aide to Carl Schurz),* Denver Pyle *(Senator Henry),* John Qualen *(Svenson),* Nanomba "Moonbeam" Morton *(Running Deer),* Dan Borzage, Dean Smith, David H. Miller, Bing Russell *(troopers).*

SYNOPSIS:

The Cheyenne Nation, living on a reservation in the desert and guarded by a cavalry unit, waits for the U.S. Government

228

representatives to fulfill their promises. After many of their people have died of starvation and disease, the Indians decide to return to their homeland. They pack up their village in the night, joined by Deborah, a Quaker woman who teaches the Indian children.

The Cheyenne are pursued by the cavalry, led by the reluctant Captain Thomas Archer. They are forced into fighting by the cavalry, but continue south in spite of cold, hunger, the cavalry, and the settlers of the land they are crossing. The Cheyenne Nation finally splits apart, with half, under Dull Knife, going to Fort Robinson for food and shelter during the winter and the rest continuing their journey, led by Little Wolf. At Fort Robinson, the Indians are locked up and starved under Captain Wessels, a Prussian commander, until they will agree to return to the reservation they left. They refuse and stage an almost suicidal escape.

Captain Archer travels to Washington to plead with the secretary of the interior on behalf of the Cheyenne. The secretary agrees that they can remain in their ancestral land, which only a fraction of their nation has reached alive.

*C*heyenne Autumn is often described as Ford's apology to the Indians he presented so one-dimensionally in his previous films. The great nobility of the Cheyenne, the absurdly evil German camp commandant, and the film's outcome, when the U.S. government reverses its decision concerning the Cheyenne, support this idea. But for a variety of reasons, this view is not very useful in an examination of John Ford's work. First, Ford has presented us with numerous noble Indians throughout his films; indeed, in almost every film in which an Indian emerges as a personality, he has as complex and compelling a personality as do the whites. Cochise of *Fort Apache* is a far more honorable man than Colonel Thursday, Scar of *The Searchers* is a mirror image of Ethan Edwards, and the intriguing old chief, Pony That Walks, in *She Wore a Yellow Ribbon* is as sensitive and well intentioned as Brittles, though not so capable.

Never are Ford's individual Indians presented as stereotypical savages. But in most of the films, the Indians represent a force that the farmers and settlers must overcome. Indians are presented, not as a hostile people, or even as hostile individuals, but as a mass. Any that emerge from the mass do so just as whites emerge from groups of farmers, townspeople, or settlers.

A second level upon which to examine *Cheyenne Autumn* in the context of Ford's work is that of point of view. In the book from which the story and title of the film were taken, the Indians' point of view is taken throughout, and the few white characters do not stand out as individuals. Ford makes no attempt to bring this point of view to the screen, seemingly acknowledging that, as a white man, he should not presume to work from an Indian sensibility. The Indians in

Making *Cheyenne Autumn.*

Cheyenne Autumn are much like the Indians of his earlier films in that they stand for something rather than being people in their own right. None, not even Spanish Woman and her son Red Shirt, are really explored on the screen to the extent that we know what makes them different from any other members of the tribe.

The lack of an Indian point of view is neither a positive nor a negative aspect. It is a reason why this work cannot be taken either as the final statement on what Ford thinks of Indians or as an apology for the so-called wrongs he has done them in the past. The film does not really involve itself with Indians except as Ford has always done — as a force of that nature which is the primitive West. What has changed is Ford's view of progress and the effect it has had on the West. This can be seen more cogently in *The Man Who Shot Liberty Valance,* in which the formal and narrative aspects are in a perfect balance not achieved in *Cheyenne Autumn.* In the very simplest of terms, the innocence the Indians symbolize has become more dear to Ford than the progress that destroys that innocence. The greater value of individualism is missing from this film, and because there is no mythical figure serving the ends of civilization, to give the struggle its transcendent quality, the "individual" of the film is represented by the Cheyenne Nation.

The visual difference between *The Man Who Shot Liberty Valance* and *Cheyenne Autumn,* as well as the reason for that difference, is apparent in the first few moments of the film. The credit sequence is shown over a gold Indian statue, behind which the background color changes from red, to deep yellow, to blue. The music is heavy and ponderous, creating with the images a feeling of foreboding. The Indians are already essentially as lost as is Tom Doniphon at the beginning of *Liberty Valance* as he lies in his coffin, for their representation is a lifeless gold statue — the legend, rather than the fact.

The first few shots immediately create a visual correlation between the Indians and the terrain of Monument Valley. The three monuments that make up the "Totem Pole" configuration are behind Spanish Woman and Red Shirt as they emerge from their tepee. They are shot in low angle and do not speak, standing as silent as the monuments behind them. Next come shots of the three chiefs of the tribe, Little Wolf, Dull Knife, and the old chief, standing in front of the three "Totem Pole" monuments, and of other Indians composed before these monuments. The narration refers to the Cheyenne as "eagles in a cage" in this desert land, but the images link them to it in their silent, waiting vigil.

The Indians, led by their chiefs, walk the long distance to the army encampment and stand in a perfect line, unmoving and unspeaking, for the entire day. Ford's framing creates an invisible line between

The Indians: each is a part of the whole of the Cheyenne Nation.

231

Relationships to the landscape: the Indians spread out over it while the Cavalry cuts into it.

the white people and the line of Indians, with Deborah's table on one side and the Indian line on the other. Even she, friend to the tribe, cannot cross the line to give the old chief water when he momentarily collapses. Thus, all the formal elements of this scene blend the Indians together, making them a mythical unity from which none stand out, except the leaders, who stand only at the head of the whole and not apart from it.

This is very much in contrast to the visual style of *Liberty Valance,* in which the dark and claustrophobic style confines the mythical qualities of the film. In *Cheyenne Autumn,* these qualities are expanded, perhaps beyond their actual value, and this is what makes the film visually unsatisfying. A quality Ford does not pretend to understand cannot fill his canvas with the power and meaning that something close to his heart does. Thus, *Cheyenne Autumn* resembles *Two Rode Together* in that the rituals seem hollow, although in the later film it seems to be not a deliberate hollowing out, but a conceptual one.

The visual representation of the Indians is in contrast to that of the cavalry in *Cheyenne Autumn,* as in earlier films. The Indians seem to be a part of the landscape; they spread out over it without cutting

into it the way a line of horse soldiers does. This difference between the cavalry and the Indians is characteristic not only of Ford, but of almost all Westerns. It represents the white view of the difference between whites and the Indians, and it provides a visual rationalization for the conquest of the West. Whites have an organized approach to life, taking over and regimenting the land itself; the Indians simply live on it. To Western sensibilities, commanding and ordering is naturally superior to living passively.

The uniformed, regimented structure of the army itself thus becomes a ritualized embodiment of this white way of living. Whenever whites are going to fight, they first turn themselves into one organized body. This is the case in *Drums Along the Mohawk,* in which a group of independent farmers, with no real allegiance except to whatever will let them live unmolested, gather at the fort and learn to march. The uniforms they eventually wear seem somehow to make them better able to defend themselves and their homes, because they restate the white man's relation to his land, in contrast with what the Indians are to the land. The whites are orderers of the environment, whereas the Indians are simply a part of it.

The attitude that has shifted from the earlier films to *Cheyenne Autumn* is not so much toward Indians as toward this structuring of the society and the land. In *Liberty Valance* Ford shows the oppressive effects of civilization on the people of the town, most obviously Hallie. While still affirming the values that make

Dodge City: a very different place from the western towns of earlier Ford Westerns, with a very different Wyatt Earp and Doc Holliday.

oppression necessary, Ford makes us all sorry for the oppressive effects on our own lives. In *Cheyenne Autumn,* the larger rationale for the whole idea of progress is lacking. Dodge City looks more like the town of *Two Rode Together* (Madame Aragon's saloon) than like Shinbone of *Liberty Valance.*

Cheyenne Autumn is a story of defeat, but rich and meaningful as that theme has always been for Ford, it is not so in this film. Gone is the fundamental belief in the values for which the defeat is suffered. In previous movies, much as Ford loves and mourns the fall of the South, his values lie with the Union and its preservation. This fundamental reference point (belief in the value of civilization, no matter

Richard Widmark: the actor does not have the strength of former Ford heroes.

235

the cost) is missing from *Cheyenne Autumn,* leaving only emptiness.

The white members of the cast are largely lacking in the force of persona Ford usually requires of his actors. Richard Widmark, who was a very adequate foil for the moral uncertainty of James Stewart in *Two Rode Together* is simply not strong enough in *Cheyenne Autumn* to carry the full weight of his dichotomous attitude toward the Indians. On the one hand, he is an army man who knew them when they were respected and feared fighters, and he does not underrate them when Deborah romanticizes the tribe. His respect is combined with a sincere desire that the promises the white leaders made to them should be kept, and for this he goes to Washington to plead the Indians' cause and gain the support of the secretary of the interior. The naïveté of Widmark's screen persona makes Tom a man of good intentions but less than wise judgment.

The Quaker woman, Deborah, with whom Tom is in love, exhibits a very naïve understanding of the Indians. She sees the future hope of their children in their reciting the English alphabet and the solution to the tribe's problems in terms of peaceful resistance. The alphabet song, a shorthand for education (the basis of democracy in a Ford Western) is a very inadequate symbol in this film. It lacks meaning because the film does not believe in what it represents. The little girl who is wounded and becomes Deborah's special charge spells out words for her, finally spelling "home" when Tom and Deborah take her to rejoin her tribe. This could be a hopeful sign for the tribe's eventual integration with the white world (which would mean their survival). But such a trivial ritual cannot stand for civilization, democracy, and education when Ford has ceased to believe in their absolute value. Thus Deborah, who demonstrates her dedication to the Cheyenne when she goes with them

Deborah: a very naive understanding of the Indians.

Tom and Deborah: their different perspectives on the Cheyenne must be worked out before they can come together.

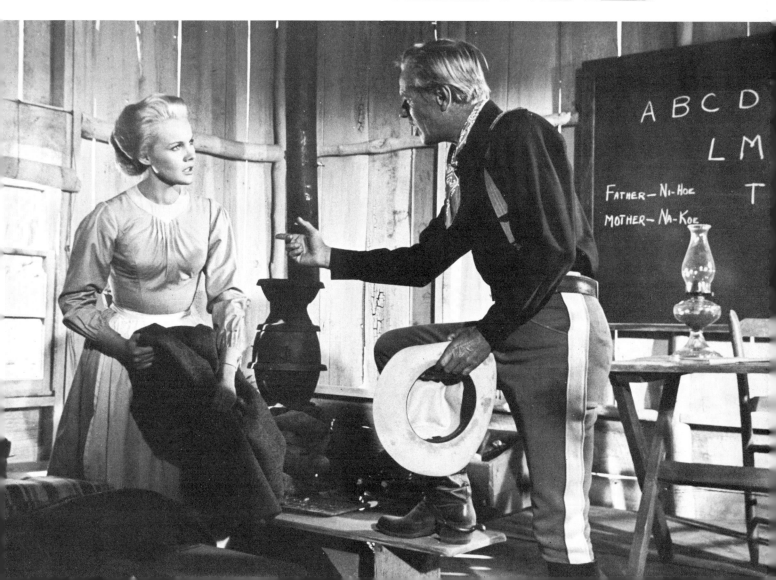

Fort Robinson: Wessels hosting a dinner for Tom and Deborah.

on their impossible march, lacks the ability to give energy and drive to the cause of education and civilization because they have become meaningless in the face of genocide. Her ridiculous naivete and commitment to values Ford previously upheld but which the film cannot believe in make explicit Ford's declining opinion of the value of Western civilization.

The little Indian girl becomes for Tom and Deborah something of what Sergeant Rutledge is for Tom and Mary—a block between them through which their racist attitudes must be worked out before they can come together as a couple. When the child is wounded by the cavalry force, lately led by Tom, Deborah is with her. Not until the little girl is healed can the couple's relationship be healed of the rupture caused by their conflicting attitudes toward the Indians.

In the "love" scene between Tom and Deborah in her schoolhouse (in which Tom tries to tell her that the Indians are savage fighters, and she insists that they are only what whites have made them), the two are separated by the rope of the school bell, which hangs between them as they talk. There is also a pole in the schoolroom that (at a different angle) comes between them, symbolizing the barrier between them. They work out their tensions on the march north. At Fort Robinson they are momentarily joined at the dinner table, when their emotions and goals seem to be the same, until the order comes to confine the Cheyenne and Wessels decides to interpret it literally. Then Deborah leaves, and Tom is prevented from being with her because of his uniform. Not until he takes it off and goes to Washington can he rejoin her emotionally. Ford's growing disillusionment with the army, expressed obviously in his portrayal of the German camp commander, is also explicitly revealed in Tom's frustration with his role. Not until Tom is ready to overstep the bounds dictated by his army oath can he really accomplish anything and, as a corollary, win the girl.

The trial at Fort Robinson:

imprisonment

breakout

aftermath

In the last scene, Tom and Deborah bring the now-healed little Indian girl home to her people, and she spells out "h-o-m-e" as they send her off to the tribe and its new home. She starts to leave, runs back for a hug from Deborah, and then leaves them for good, removing the barrier between Tom and Deborah that she has represented. It seems almost an upbeat moment, for the tribe is again joined and the lovers are finally together emotionally. The spelling ritual seems to affirm the value that has not been lost through the ordeal, and the little girl seems the embodiment of hope for the future of the tribe.

This farewell, however, is as unredeemed an ending as Ford has ever had in a Western. The joining of the lovers is the only value to it, and they are so uncompelling, both as lovers and as a positive force in the film, that to juxtapose their moment of happiness with the unrelieved tragedy of the Cheyenne borders on black comedy. The worst possible tragedy that could befall the tribe is to be torn apart. In the march north, this happens—the tribe splits, and the force it represents is destroyed. No longer is the tribe one entity that can remain vital as long as any remnant of it survives.

This destruction is made explicit when Little Wolf kills Red Shirt. A Cheyenne leader's only proper concern is for the safety of his people, and no Cheyenne may take the life of another Cheyenne and remain in the tribe. This act of violence breaks many ties—those of family, of tribe, and of tribal mythology—that it can never be made right. The leader who brought them to this new place, where they might have some chance of surviving as a people, is forced (by honor, as well as by his feelings as a man) to destroy that chance. The breach caused by this one act is more final than anything the whites could do to them. It represents a permanent split in the tribe that could come from nothing short of the failure of its values to prevail over those of the corrupting white civilization. Their values are those of the innocent West, and their ultimate defeat at their own hands is a denial of the worth of those values.

The character of Red Shirt is the most interesting of the tribe, even though in the extant version of the film his part has been pared down to a ghost of what it was intended to be. He appears in the first scene, emerging from his tepee in a bright red shirt, the color immediately signifying danger, but also sexual potency and vitality. He is anxious for a fight, and he will not submit to the whites; and his action and the response to it ruin the tribe. But he is more a force than an individual, and his actions are part of the collective psyche of the tribe. He represents a spark and vitality that will not admit defeat, and it is significant in a Ford film that not only does he die, but his death marks the ultimate defeat of the tribe, a defeat that could not have been brought about externally but had to come from the very heart of the tribe itself.

240

Red Shirt begins the firing on the U.S. Cavalry.

241

The death of the old chief and the passage of leadership.

Little Wolf, Dull Knife, and Red Shirt: the tribe splits apart.

If one likens the split of the tribe to the dissolution of a family, then *Cheyenne Autumn* becomes an abstract, schematized *How Green Was My Valley*. In *Valley* the tragedy of the father's death (the final step in the breakdown of the family that began with the leaving of four brothers and the death of another) is filtered through the sensibilities of the son, who is telling the story, but such an interpretive process does not take place in *Cheyenne Autumn*. This is what leaves the later film so absolutely unredeemed. In Ford's earlier films, suffering and defeat had to be endured for a reason—they became a ritual that affirmed all who experienced them, through the one character who stood apart from the community. In *Cheyenne Autumn* the tragedy becomes an all-pervasive negative feeling, with no center to give it transcendent value.

For the little Indian girl to spell out "h-o-m-e" as she joins her tribe is an abstraction of any real home, either for her and her people or for the world of film. She has returned to a split tribe, living in slightly better surroundings than before, with more than half of its people dead. She is an orphan, and for Ford, lack of an immediate family carries connotations of a lack of personal center. This is what the tribe has lost, and this little orphan's return "home" is as bleak as when the boy leaves the valley in *How Green Was My Valley,* but with no individual sensibility to relieve it.

Cheyenne Autumn is ultimately a nihilist statement. No individual in the narrative has the power to determine any aspect of his life, least of all the Indians, who starve, even die, finally to get one tiny portion of what they have been promised, and then only through the grace of Tom and the secretary of the interior. Tom and Deborah are impotent characters, she in her naivete, which sees the Cheyenne only as children, and he with his "duty," which serves no one but the cattle and land interests.

Secretary Schurz fears that his benevolent action will simply give his enemies "the false move they are waiting for." He is a pitiful character, sitting in his big office, from which he must escape to find even a little peace and any correct information. He seems a representation of Ford's disenchantment with the growing bureaucracy of democracy that prevents even people of power from carrying out their best ideas. The secretary's powerlessness is made poignant by his contrast with one of Ford's greatest American heroes, Abraham Lincoln. They are formally joined when Schurz's worried face is reflected in the framed portrait of Lincoln, and we feel that Schurz's is not a personal failure but that conditions make honorable decisions impossible. It is significant that in many of his late films *(The Quiet Man, Mogambo, Mister Roberts, Donovan's Reef, Young Cassidy,* and finally *Seven Women)* Ford chose to go outside the United States for his locale, thus avoiding the questions he must come to terms with in *The Man Who Shot*

Spanish Woman, Deborah, and the wounded Cheyenne girl.

Secretary of the Interior Carl Schurz: his act in favor of the Cheyenne may be the "one false move" his enemies are waiting for.

Liberty Valance and *Cheyenne Autumn.* He deals with the same broad questions in all these films, but since he must situate the Westerns in the United States, the questions become more compelling because Ford seems to have lost faith in the past he created in his earlier Westerns.

The lack of power, especially the power (or even existence) of the individual, is in contrast with every other Ford film, including his last, *Seven Women,* which is also very black and nihilistic, but gives us a character with whom to identify and through whom to experience the film. In the final analysis, this is what makes *Cheyenne Autumn* unsatisfying. Even in his most pessimistic statements, Ford works through the sensibilities of an individual, usually a person who functions apart from the group but remains allied with it in some way. When that individual is lacking, the ritualistic process of affirming the experience of the film does not take place.

There are many traditionally Fordian moments and characters in *Cheyenne Autumn* that lack the impact of those in earlier films because there is no individual through whom to experience them. Most obvious is the comedy centered around stock Fordian characters. Since there is no leader with the force of John Wayne or the ambiguity and power of James Stewart, the bit players have no focal point for their comedy. The top sergeant does manage a very moving and illuminating scene with Tom when he thinks his enlistment is up and plans to leave the next morning. He tells his former commanding officer about his native Russia, where the Cossacks terrorize people who are just trying to live peacefully. He admits his feeling that the American cavalry is now in the role of those Cossacks, while he is careful not to question their earlier role as tamers of the West.

Tom is powerless to do anything but understand the man's feeling, and his impotent truth is raised to the level of existential statement when Wichowsky decides to reenlist after all, because he has nothing better to do. As in *What Price Glory?* the question is no longer justice, but simple affirmation of one's dedication to a purpose, even if one acknowledges that purpose to be hollow. Wichowsky remains faithful just to be faithful, just to affirm what he is, and not to do justice. This is a broader and more complex concept that in retrospect sheds light on Colonel Thursday of *Fort Apache* and on Ford's whole concept of duty and the limits to which Ford is willing to take it.

Visually, the Cheyenne are linked with a past and a predestination that is at the heart of Ford's maturing vision. When they leave the reservation, the cavalry catches up with them just as they are crossing the river, and we experience this in an unusual and almost awkward panning shot from the cavalry on one side of the river to the Indians just in the final stages of crossing it. It is a moment of doom, foreshadowed by the unexpected camera movement, which is unsettling

The Cheyenne during their impossible march.

both in its formal qualities and in its implication of things done that cannot be undone.

The old chief's funeral in the rocks is similar—the ritual looks back to meaning, instead of forward to a joined community as do the rituals of earlier films. When the Indians expect to find buffalo and find only bones left by the hide hunters, the sky looks very strange and unreal—it is gray on blue in an otherworldly canvas that makes the Cheyenne appear lost in time as well as in space. In the last scene, in which Little Wolf and his wife ride off toward the horizon, having broken the most sacred oath of the tribe and now irreparably cut off from them, the visual line is a down-sloping diagonal. The premonitions of doom, conveyed by the credit sequence, have been realized.

The Cheyenne represent the most powerful and compelling force in *Cheyenne Autumn;* yet they are doomed to defeat. Here is the final despair of the movie; even the mythical, tribal spirit of a people with a glorious history of ritual, victory, and honor, determined to control their own destiny, cannot survive. The tribe lives through an impossible march of starvation and the loss of most of its members, and then, at the end of its struggle, it cannot hold itself together. That the split comes from inside is a last symbol of the hopelessness of their future. They are not conquered but, like Tom Doniphon, destroy themselves with conflicting internal forces. In contrast with *Liberty Valance,* however, no redeeming unity comes from their sacrifice. The myth is exposed as inadequate. The search for meaning in life has become absurd.

Tom and Deborah bring the now-healed Cheyenne girl "home."

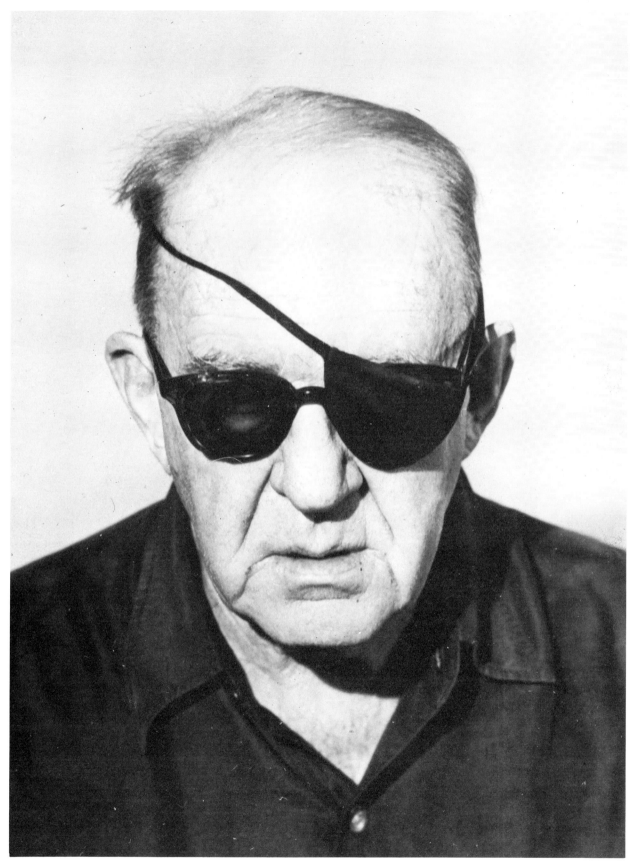

John Ford.